MACRAMÉ
made easy

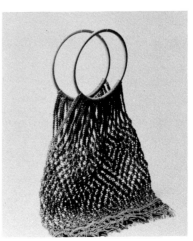

MACRAMÉ
made easy

Eunice Close

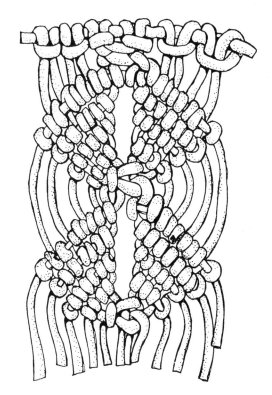

Collier Books

Division of Macmillan Publishing Co., Inc.

New York

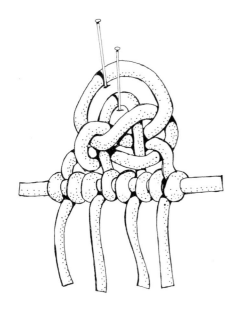

Macmillan Publishing Co., Inc.

866 Third Avenue, New York, N.Y. 10022

Library of Congress Catalog Card Number 73-4055.

First Printing 1973

Printed in Great Britain

Contents

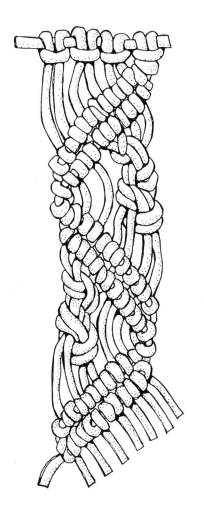

Introducing macramé

a brief history of the craft

Macramé is one of those crafts which looks a good deal more complicated than it actually is. In fact, anyone who is capable of tying a piece of string round a parcel should be able to make any of the articles described in this book.

The art or craft of macramé is, in essence, the making of useful articles or decorative designs by means of knotting together some kind of string or thread. This may be as thick as quite heavy string or thin rope or as fine as crochet cotton. It is an ancient craft whose origins go so far back into history that no one quite knows where or how it began. It is generally assumed, however, that it first appeared somewhere in the Middle East, probably in the lands surrounding the valleys of the Tigris and Euphrates. The history of this area during the pre-Christian era is one of constant change as one nation declined and another took its place. Throughout the period, nevertheless, a high standard of civilization appears to have been reached, as was also the case in the highly sophisticated culture of the Egypt of that time.

A good deal of evidence in support of this has come down to us in the form of statues, carvings, paintings and all kinds of objects fashioned from precious stones and metals. Unfortunately, such things as clothing and hangings used in furnishing have, by the nature of the materials from which they were made, completely disappeared, so that we can only find reference to their existence from statues and carvings which have survived. We are therefore justified in assuming that macramé was a highly developed craft as far back as 3000 B.C. or even earlier.

It must have been at a very early stage in man's development that the need arose for tying things together and at first, no doubt, use was made of the strong stems of climbing plants or strips hacked from the skins of the animals that primitive man hunted and killed.

Once someone had discovered how to spin and weave, a much more complicated and sophisticated life became possible. As conditions became easier and more settled, the urge to make the environment more beautiful, as well as more comfortable, began to make itself felt. At first these embellishments may have been simple fringes cut along the edges of a garment or curtain. Gradually, as skill in weaving increased they could have progressed to a fringe made by unravelling the edge of the material. From there it would have been a short step to knotting the strands to form simple and, later, more elaborate patterns. Then, perhaps, someone realized that it was a waste of time to weave a piece of cloth only to unravel it again. The material was dispensed with and the threads already spun could be used to make even more elaborate designs.

It is interesting to note in this connection that the development of macramé closely resembles that of both bobbin- and needle-made laces and that these crafts also appear to have originated in the Middle East. One of the most important features of the civilization of this period was the flourishing commerce which was carried on all over the Mediterranean. There was in consequence a vigorous exchange of ideas as well as of goods, and the knowledge and practice of crafts of all kinds was spread over a wide area.

Another important influence in the spread of knowledge about macramé was the work of the sailors who manned the fleets of merchant ships which were continually passing up and down the great trade routes. Obviously these men would have a great deal to do with the tying of knots since using ropes would constitute a large part of their work. They would use what spare time they had to make useful and decorative articles from the materials which lay at hand. This tradition lasted through hundreds of years right down to the time when sailing ships were ousted by steam. Indeed, it is likely that it is still carried on in some parts of the world. Only a year or so ago someone showed me a most attractive belt which she was wearing. It was worked in macramé in fine twine and had been bought from a sailor.

Coming now to more modern times, we know that in the fifteenth and sixteenth centuries lacemaking and its associated craft of macramé became very popular in many parts of Europe. It was a period of great richness in dress and house decoration and the elaborate patterns it was possible to make in macramé fitted in well with the prevailing fashions.

The popularity of macramé, like that of lace, has always been subject to fluctuation and there have been periods when the craft might have been thought to be completely lost. Fortunately, however, some of the European convents, particularly those in

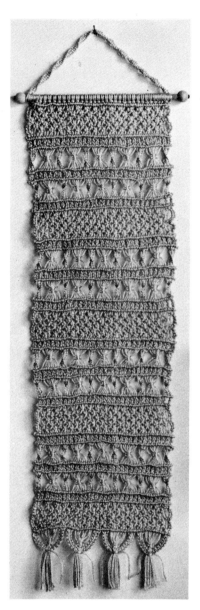

Instructions for this wall hanging start on page 49

7

Italy, went on teaching the craft, as well as producing all kinds of ecclesiastical garments and furnishings. Very few examples of this kind of work seem to have survived and one seldom finds examples of macramé in museums. The Victoria and Albert Museum in London has some pieces of Italian work dating from the late sixteenth and early seventeenth centuries and some which they think may be English.

In Victorian times, in England, macramé again staged a revival. It was one of the "accomplishments" which all young ladies were supposed to possess and it fitted in well with the Victorian fondness for heavy and ornate trimmings in their over-decorated homes. It was used to edge blinds and what I believe were called mantel borders, as well as for antimacassars and for the mats which had to cover every flat surface.

During the first half of this century there was a violent reaction against Victorian ideas which led to the sweeping away of everything that was thought to be over-ornate. Naturally, macramé and all it represented was one of the first things to disappear and one might have thought it would have been lost for ever. However, someone somewhere always seems to remember these things.

In the last few years the pendulum seems to be swinging back and fashions in house decoration are becoming much less severe. A new interest is being taken in crafts of all kinds, perhaps in reaction against the highly technical age in which we live. Macramé, in common with lacemaking, is sharing in this revival.

All the designs which appear on the following pages have been designed specially for this book. I have kept in mind throughout the need to adapt such designs so that they will fit happily into the environment of the present day. Although some of the designs to be found in the old instruction books are attractive and intricate, I feel that many of them are too fussy for modern tastes so, although I have used all the traditional knots, I have tried to interpret them in a modern way. In this I have, of course, been helped by the great number of new kinds of threads which have appeared on the market during the last few years.

Some of the designs are intended for use in the home, others can be used for dress accessories and most of them can be easily adapted for purposes other than those described. You will find all of them quite simple to make provided you follow the instructions carefully. Where necessary, I have included directions for making up, as well as working the articles, and I have used only those materials which are readily obtainable. Macramé combines very happily with knitting and crochet and in one or two cases you will find that I have included these in the same article.

Basic equipment and materials

The tools needed for making macramé – in addition to your own fingers which are the principal tools you will use – are those which can be found in any household. The main items are a pair of strong, sharp scissors, a tape measure and a supply of strong pins with large heads. Those with coloured heads, obtainable from any large department store, are the best kind to use, although ordinary pins with a blob of sealing wax fixed to the head will serve the purpose just as well. An ordinary ruler is useful for measuring fringes while a string needle and a supply of large tapestry needles will be helpful for fastening off. If you wish to work out your own designs a supply of graph paper and a few coloured pencils may be added to your list.

Sometimes a macramé border is worked into the edge of a piece of material or into a crochet chain and for this you will need a crochet hook. The size of this will, of course, depend on the thickness of the thread you are using. It must be large enough to hold the thread but not so large as to tear the material. A hook is also needed when cords have to be added as the work progresses, as may occur when the design is a circular one, particularly if you are using a fine thread. A pair of C clamps such as those used for holding a table-tennis net is useful but not essential. The clamps can be used for measuring when a large number of cords has to be cut or they can act as supports to which the cords can be fixed while the knots are being made.

Before a piece of macramé is started it must be fastened to something firm. The C clamp already mentioned, a convenient hook or door knob or even the back of a chair can be used, but if you wish to get the best results it is worth your while to make a special support. None of the following is difficult to make nor are the materials from which they are made expensive or difficult to

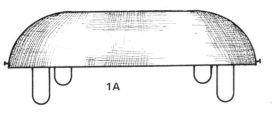

1A

1B

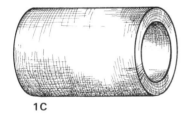

1C

obtain. Figure 1 shows three pillows which are suitable for working most of the designs shown in this book. 1A is the conventional French shape while 1B and 1C are lacemaking pillows.

To make the pillow shown in 1A you will need a piece of wood approximately 18 inches by 7 inches by $\frac{1}{2}$ inch, one piece of closely woven material such as sail cloth 22 inches by 10 inches and a second piece 19 inches by 8 inches, four plastic doorstops and some kind of padding material. I find the artificial horsehair sold for upholstery both effective and reasonable in price. A piece of foam rubber about 1 inch thick makes a good base for this kind of padding. Place the latter, cut to fit, on the wood base with a thick layer of padding on top. Over this lay the larger piece of material, turn the surplus over on to the underside of the wood and fix it in place with plenty of thumb tacks or upholstery tacks, pulling the material as tightly as possible and adding more padding if necessary to make a really firm pillow. Neaten the back by turning in the edges of the second piece of material and tacking it over the base. Finally, screw one of the doorstops into each corner of the base of the pillow. The plastic ends prevent the pillow from slipping and protect the surface on which the cushion stands.

The circular pillow shown in Figure 1B is made in exactly the same way but has no feet. I used a 12-inch circular tray base as a foundation but a larger pillow can be made if required by cutting out a larger circle of wood or plasterboard.

The bolster-shaped pillow shown in Figure 1C is very useful when you are making a long piece of macramé such as a braid or a belt. This is one is stuffed with sawdust. Take a piece of strong material about 16 inches by 24 inches and join the long sides to make a tube. Cut two circles of thick cardboard, hardboard or thin plywood to fit tightly inside the tube. Using very strong thread gather one end of the tube and push one circle of cardboard well down inside it. Fill the tube with sawdust packing it in as firmly as you can. It is a good idea to leave it overnight to settle. Push the second circle of cardboard well down on top of the sawdust and gather the open end. Sew a circle of material over the raw edges to make a neat finish. A washable cover can be made for any of these pillows by hemming a piece of material several inches larger all round and inserting a length of elastic.

If you wish to make a large piece of macramé such as a rug or wall hanging, the pillows may be too small. In this case you can use a large drawing board, or even the kitchen table padded with a folded blanket secured with upholstery tacks.

Although it is quite possible to join on extra lengths of thread during working it is better to avoid this as much as possible. Most macramé designs are worked with very long threads. Various methods can be used to prevent them from becoming tangled while the work is in progress. The simplest way is to wind each cord round your fingers and to secure the loops with an elastic band.

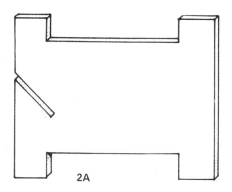

2A

Small cards cut as shown in Figure 2A can also be used. The cardboard from which they are made must be fairly substantial as the holders undergo a lot of handling and thin card soon becomes torn. A shoebox or similar container provides a good source of suitable cardboard. Wind the cord evenly round the center of the card and slip through the slit in the side.

More permanent thread holders can be made quite simply as shown in Figure 2B. The main section is about $2\frac{1}{2}$ inches long and is cut from a piece of dowel rod or a plastic knitting needle. The ends are cut from a piece of larger dowel rod glued or nailed in place or from wooden button molds. After winding on the thread secure it with a knot as shown in Figure 2C. This prevents the thread from unwinding as you work but allows you to lengthen it as required.

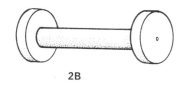

2B

When we come to the question of the materials used for macramé it is difficult to know where to begin, for the number and kinds of threads that are available is almost endless. The traditional material, of course, is string of some kind. This may be made from jute, hemp, flax or wool and, nowadays, in addition, from one of the many man-made fibers now available in bewildering variety. A visit to a shop selling rope and string will yield a wide choice of threads and you will often find that their goods are cheaper than those bought in a hardware or stationery store. Most of the material will be in what is known as natural shades which means that they will range in colour from almost pure white to a quite dark, greyish-brown shade. However, there is no reason why they should not be dyed to whatever colour you need, although you may have to experiment a little to obtain what you want. It is better, I think, to wind the string into hanks and dye it before use rather than to dye the finished article.

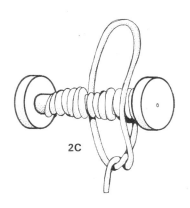

2C

Handicraft shops are now stocking several types of cord specially for macramé work and new types are appearing all the time. They usually include a fairly heavy cord available in several good colours and a softer cord in black, cream and white. Both of these are suitable for such articles as shopping bags.

Any needlework shop will provide many kinds of thread suitable for macramé work. They include the usual mercerised crochet cottons in many colours and thicknesses and most of these can be used for the finer designs. A strong thread called heavy stitching thread works up well and there are many types of rayon knitting

This evening bag, worked in a silky knitting thread, is made from a simple pattern which is easily adapted for other purposes. Instructions are on page 44

thread which can be used for macramé. A look round the needle-work department of a large store should provide plenty of choice. A thick, fluffy type of thread is also sold specially for macramé and this works up well and quickly. This type of thread has the advantage of being loosely twisted from three strands which can be unwound and used singly if required.

Wool can be used very successfully provided it is firmly twisted and not too fine. Double knitting wool comes in many colours and varieties and those which are of man-made fibers are particularly good for making articles in macramé. A hard-wearing tapestry wool is useful for making braids. Incidentally, if you have difficulty in obtaining furnishing braid to match a piece of wool embroidery or tapestry, a braid worked in macramé from the wool you have been using may solve your problem.

Cotton seining twine or white braided rayon or nylon cord that you can dye may be found in hardware stores or obtained in a variety of colours from macramé suppliers. You might also check millinery suppliers or drapery and upholstery shops for interesting materials. Possible choices include knotting yarn and rug wook, silk braid, thick Lurex thread, upholsterer's cord, parachute braid (from Army/Navy stores), polypropylene and other synthetic cords.

This does not by any means exhaust the list of possible materials for macramé. Once you have begun this fascinating craft you will find yourself eyeing every piece of string or ball of thread that comes your way, wondering whether you could use it for macramé. Some threads may prove unsuitable but others may be unexpectedly successful, so do not be afraid to experiment with whatever threads or yarns you may happen to find.

The curtain tie was worked in contrasting threads to give a textured finish. Instructions are on page 73

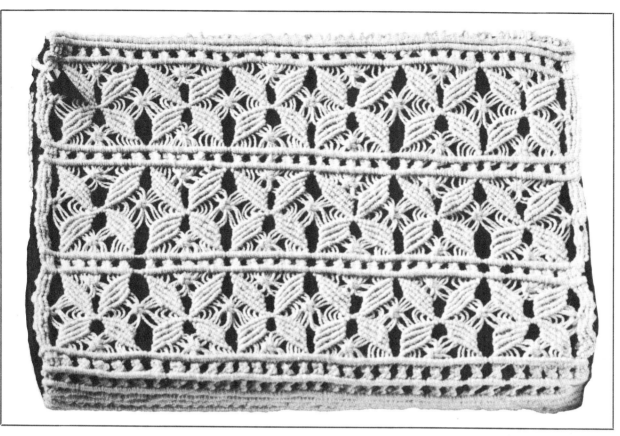

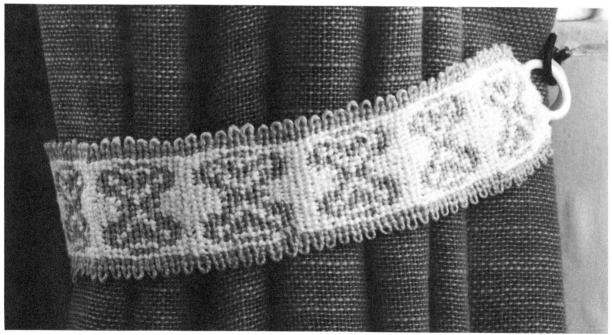

Explaining the terms
and a guide to the basic knots

Before you begin to learn the basic knots used in all macramé work you will need to know the terms used throughout this book.

Strings

I use this term to describe the lengths of string, thread or wool from which the macramé article is made. Thus, if the instructions state: "Cut x strings each y inches long," you will know that this means the total length needed for that particular piece of work. It is generally assumed that the strings should be eight or nine times the length of the finished piece but I find that this is not always enough. In any case the amount may vary considerably according to the type and thickness of the thread being used. A thick bulky string will take more in proportion to its size than will a thin one.

Cords

When a string is attached to a foundation of some kind it has to be folded, generally in half, but sometimes with one end longer than the other. After being knotted on to a foundation the string becomes a pair of cords. These cords are of two kinds—knotting cords and holding cords. The former are those *with* which the knots are made and the latter those *on* which the knots are made. They are interchangeable in that the same piece of cord may become either a knotting or holding cord as the pattern requires. Should the instructions state: "Knot on x pairs of cords," each string counts as one pair. In many cases the strings are knotted on to a separate piece of string, often one which is slightly thicker than that used for the main part of the work. This is known as the foundation cord.

Braids

When a series of knots has to be worked with the same group of cords I shall refer to the resulting strip as a braid.

Tension

It should be noted that where I have drawn diagrams showing how the various knots are tied I have made these appear to be much more loosely worked than they actually are. This has been done purposely in order to make the method of working quite clear. When they are being worked the cords must be pulled firmly and the knots must lie closely side by side. Most workers soon develop their own speed and tension of working and once this has been attained you should be able to work an even piece of macramé that is neither so loosely worked as to be limp nor so tightly done as to become puckered.

Knotting on

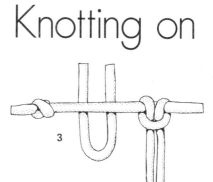

3

This is the term used for attaching the cords to a foundation of some kind. This may be the foundation cord already mentioned, the edge of a piece of material, a length of crochet chain or a wooden or plastic ring. The simplest form of knotting on is shown in Figure 3. First fix a foundation cord to your pillow by tying a knot in each end and pushing a strong pin through each knot so that the cord is stretched tightly between them. Fold a string in half and place the loop downwards under the foundation cord. Bring the ends over the cord and through the loop pulling them gently until the small bar is close to the foundation and the ends hang down. The same method is used when the cords have to be knotted on to a piece of material or a crochet edging except that the loop is drawn through from front to back with the aid of a crochet hook. Occasionally it may be necessary to reverse this process, so that the little bar made by the loop lies at the back of the work. Knotting on can also be done with a decorative heading using picots, single or double chains or scallops, but as these involve a knowledge of several basic knots I will deal with them towards the end of this chapter.

Flat knot

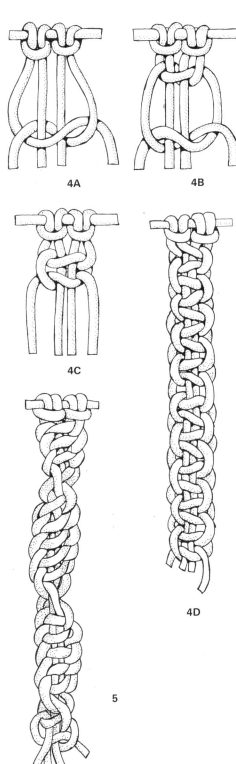

4A   4B

4C

4D

5

The flat knot is one of the most frequently used knots in macramé. In its simplest form it requires four cords (i.e. two pairs) although it can be made with more when the pattern requires it. You may see it referred to as Solomon's Knot, not to be confused with the crochet stitch bearing the same name, Solomon's Bar, square knot or sennit. Each flat knot consists of two movements worked alternately. It does not matter which half is worked first, provided you keep to the same order throughout a piece of work. In order to avoid confusion I have kept to the same order all through this book.

To make a flat knot, knot on two strings so that you have two pairs of cords hanging from your foundation cord. Note that the two cords in the center are not actually tied and should be kept as taut as possible. You may find it helpful to pin them to your pillow. Take the right hand cord and pass it under the center cords and over the left hand cord, at the same time bringing the left hand cord over the center cords and under the right hand cord. Draw up the cords gently so that they lie neatly just below the knotting on (Figure 4A). Now reverse this movement, taking the left hand cord under the center pair and over the right hand cord, at the same time bringing the right hand cord over the center cords and under the left hand cord (Figure 4B). Tighten the knot as before so that it looks like Figure 4C and 4D. Flat knots may be worked singly or repeated as many times as required.

Sometimes a half flat knot only is worked. It may be either the first or second half—either Figure 4A repeated or 4B repeated—so long as the same one is used throughout. You will find that the resulting braid will twist itself into a spiral and, as this may become a little difficult to control, the center cords should be pinned down very firmly. You will find it helpful, too, to pin the braid down the sides at intervals of 1 inch or so, so that the braid will not become twisted until the end of the particular section is reached (Figure 5). These braids make strong and attractive bag handles.

There are many variations of flat knots and most of them are incorporated in one or more of the designs shown on the following pages. They include flat knots with picots or overhand knots, flat knots over four or six threads, and flat knots with shells. The latter are simply overhand hand knots using the two center cords and worked between each two flat knots.

This simple and flattering vest can be adapted to fit any size. Instructions start on page 62

A square, linen mat with a macramé lace border. Instructions are on page 80

Half hitch

We come now to the half hitch, which is the simplest and most frequently used knot you will need. It can be worked in two directions, according to whether you are working from left to right or vice versa. It is always worked by a knotting cord on a holding cord. At the beginning of a design the foundation cord frequently becomes the holding cord.

Figure 6A shows a half hitch which is worked with the right hand (knotting) cord on the left hand (holding) cord. In this case the holding cord is held in the right hand on top of the knotting cord and the knot is made with the left hand. Figure 6B shows the knot worked in the opposite direction and here the holding cord is held in the left hand while the knot is tied with the right. Remember that the holding cord must always be on top. If you make a series of half hitches in either of these two directions the result will again be a spiral.

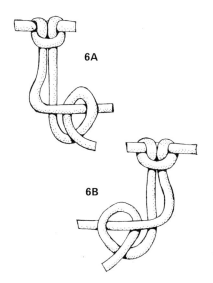

Single and double chains

A single chain is made as shown in Figure 7A and 7B. From this you will see that the half hitches are worked alternately right on left, then left on right. A double chain is worked in exactly the same way except that four cords are used and the knots are worked with double cords which must lie neatly side by side (Figure 7C and 7D).

A delicate doily that would look equally well on a dressing table or dining table. Instructions are on page 78

Bars

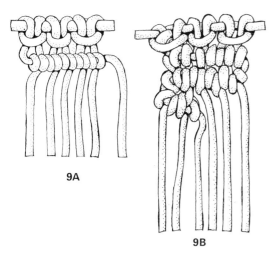

8A

8B

9A

9B

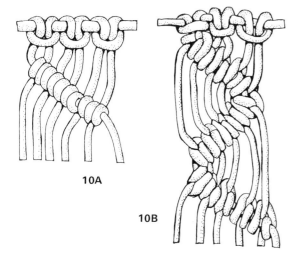

10A

10B

One of the most noticeable features of macramé is the use of bars. These may be horizontal, slanting or vertical and they are always worked with a series of half hitches worked in pairs. Two half hitches do not, as might be supposed, make one whole hitch but are known as a double half hitch or clove hitch. A double half hitch is made as shown in Figures 8A and 8B, the former being worked from left to right, the latter from right to left.

A horizontal bar is made as shown in Figure 9A. Working from left to right, hold the first cord on the left across the other cords. Then, with the left hand, made a double half hitch with each cord in turn. When working from right to left simply reverse the procedure (Figure 8B). Figure 9B shows a horizontal bar worked in each direction.

A slanting bar (Figures 10A and 10B) is worked in exactly the same way except that the holding cord is held downwards at an angle across the other cords. Slanting bars may be joined by being crossed but there are so many ways of doing this that I shall mention them as they occur in a particular design.

Vertical bars are slightly different from the other two in that the knotting cord is continuous while the other cords serve in turn as holding cords. For this reason the knotting cord must be a very long one as it becomes used up very quickly (Figures 11A and 11B).

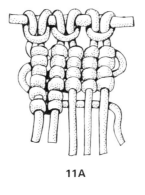

11A

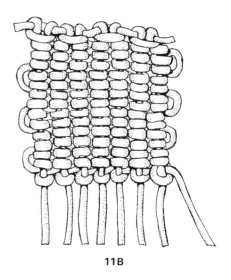

11B

This fringed wall hanging can be adapted to a wider or narrower width to suit your room. Instructions start on page 49

Overhand knots

12

These are made as shown in Figure 12 and may be worked with one or more cords as required. They are useful in tying off cords to make a fringe.

Reversed double half hitch

13B

This is very similar to the stitch used in tatting and is worked as shown in Figures 13A and 13B. This uses only two cords but an attractive variation is shown in Figure 13C. As you will see this uses four cords and the reversed double half hitches are worked alternately with the two outer cords.

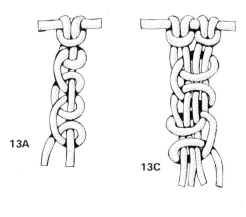

13A

13C

To make this useful shopping bag you will need string, available in different colours, and wooden or plastic handles. There are three alternative methods of making the base. Instructions start on page 34

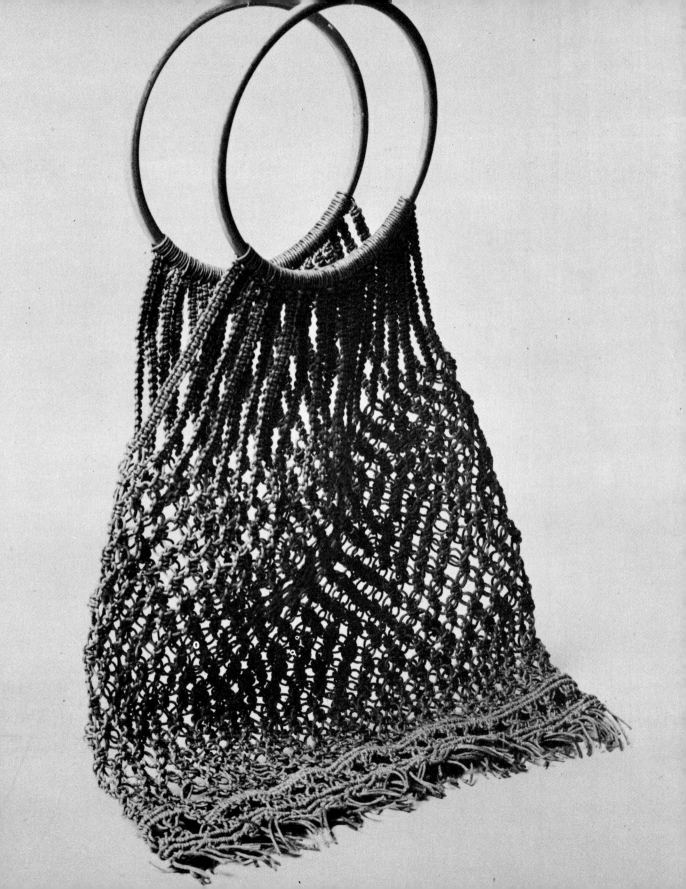

Variations in knotting on

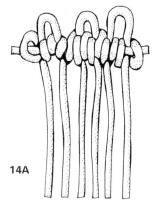

14A

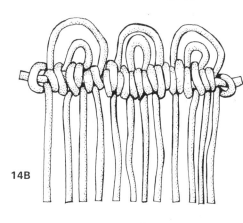

14B

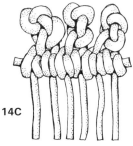

14C

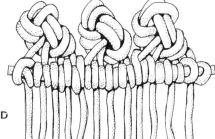

14D

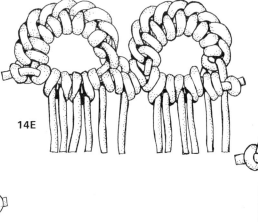

14E

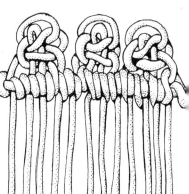

14F

Figures 14A to F show six ways of knotting on which can be used to give a decorative border to a piece of work. All of them require a foundation cord on which is worked a horizontal bar. Figures 15A and 15B show two simple picot edgings. A foundation cord is pinned to the pillow and the first string is folded in half and the loop pinned above the foundation with the ends going underneath. Then make a double half hitch over the foundation cord with each of the knotting cords. Continue in this way until the required number of cords has been knotted. The double picot is made in exactly the same way but using four cords.

Figure 16 shows a picot combined with a flat knot. It requires four cords, the center pair being pinned in place to form a rather long picot while the outer cords are used to make a flat knot round it.

Figures 17A and 17B are worked with a single and double chain respectively. Each chain consists of only two half hitches which are tied in the center of the string. Pin the knot to the pillow above the foundation cords and work a horizontal bar.

Figure 18 shows a method which is a little more complicated. Knot on four strings in reverse. Then, using the right hand cord of the first pair on the left as a holding cord, make a series of half hitches with the left hand cord of the same pair. The number of knots may very according to the thickness of the thread you are using but the scallop should be long enough to curve over the foundation cord in a semi-circle. Finish by working a double half hitch on the foundation cord using the two cords with which you have worked the scallop.

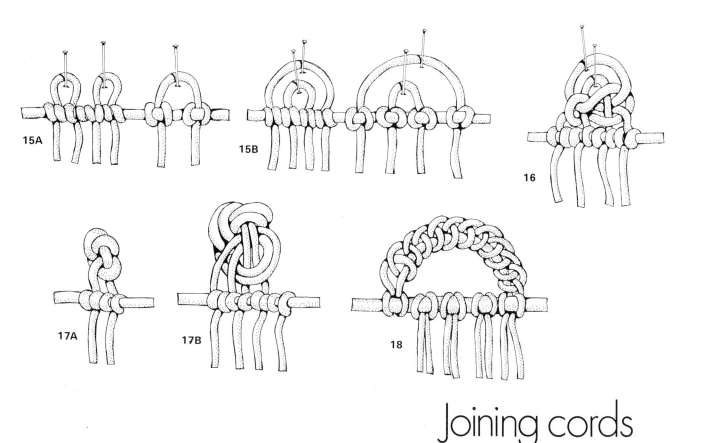

15A 15B 16

17A 17B 18

Joining cords

As I have already mentioned, macramé is usually worked with very long threads but occasions do arise when you find that a cord is not long enough. String can be spliced by unravelling the ends of the old and new pieces and twisting half the strands of each together. A little fabric glue may be used to keep them in place. Threads may also be tied neatly at the back of the work where they will not show.

Fastening off

The finishing of a piece of work often presents something of a problem since there are so many ends to be disposed of. There are several ways in which this can be done neatly and decoratively and you will find details in the instructions for making each article.

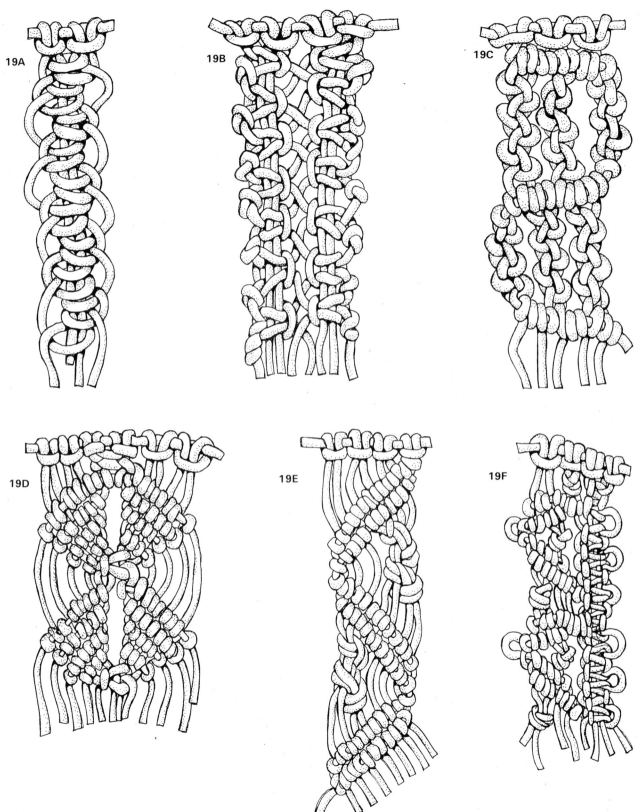

19A

19B

19C

19D

19E

19F

26

Simple braids to give you practice

Figures 19A to F show a selection of six simple braids for you to try, to give you some practice in working some of the knots already described.

Figure 19A is a very simple braid which requires only four cords. It is a variation of a double half hitch in which the knots are made over the two center cords using the left and right cords alternately.

Figure 19B is a little more complicated and requires four pairs of cords, i.e., two pairs for each half of the pattern. Knot the pairs on to a foundation cord. Make a flat knot as shown in Figure 4C with the two pairs on the right, then make an overhand knot with the cord on the extreme right. Leave these cords and make a flat knot with the two pairs on the left, but this time reverse the order of working the two halves so that the first half is worked as shown in Figure 4B and the second half as Figure 4A. Tie an overhand knot with the cord on the left, cross the two inside cords left over right and repeat from the beginning for the length required.

Figure 19C has three pairs of cords knotted on to a foundation cord. Using the left hand cord as a holding cord make a horizontal bar going from left to right and using each of the other five cords in turn. Make a single chain consisting of six half hitches worked alternately with each pair. Using the right hand cord make a horizontal bar as before, this time working from right to left. Make a single chain of six half hitches with each pair. Repeat for length required.

Figure 19D requires six pairs of cords knotted on to a foundation cord. Make a flat knot with the four cords in the center. Using the sixth cord from the left as a holding cord make a bar of five double half hitches slanting downwards to the left. Still using the sixth cord from the left (this was formerly the fifth one) make a bar immediately below the first one, this time making four double half hitches. In the same way make two more bars of three and two double half hitches respectively. Using the sixth cord from the right as a holding cord make a similar triangle of four bars this time sloping to the right. Repeat from beginning for length required. You will notice that the threads left between the triangles make attractive open triangles down each side.

Figure 19E requires four pairs of cords knotted on to a foundation cord. Using the cord on the extreme right make a bar slanting to the left with the other seven cords. Still using the cord on the extreme right (this was used for the first double half hitch of the previous bar) make a second bar of seven double half hitches close to the first. Note that in contrast to the previous braid the cord on the left which was the holding cord for the first bar is used to make the seventh double half hitch. Make a double chain of four knots with the two right hand pairs. Now, using the cord on the extreme left as the holding cord make a slanting bar to the right with a second bar immediately below it and using all seven cords as before. Make a double chain of four knots with the two pairs on the left. Repeat from the beginning for the length required. This braid would be very effective as a finish to a stool or chair seat worked in tapestry, especially if the wool used for the canvas work were also used for the braid.

Figure 19F requires four pairs of cords. Worked with a fine thread, it would make a dainty edging for a handkerchief. As it has a picot edging down each side it must be worked on a pillow. Start by making two flat knots with the two pairs on the right. Using the two cords on the extreme left together make an overhand knot. With the fourth cord from the right as a holding cord make a slanting bar consisting of four double half hitches. Using the fifth from the right as a holding cord make a bar immediately below the first consisting of three double half hitches. Make an overhand knot with the third and fourth cords from the left used double. Place a pin a little to the left of the last bar worked and take the holding cord round the pin to form a picot. Using the same cord make a bar slanting to the right using the next three cords. Go back to the right hand side and place a pin to the right of the last flat knot. Bring the right hand cord round the pin to form a picot, then work two flat knots, make another picot and two more flat knots. Work a fourth slanting bar close to the third one using the cord on the left as a holding cord and working four double half hitches. Note that the last of these is worked with the left hand cord of those used for the flat knots. Make another picot on the right and repeat from the beginning.

Two belts

Macramé is an excellent medium for making belts, so here are instructions for making two. The first is in a rather soft string sold specially for macramé and the second is made from silky crochet thread.

Belt with toggle fastening

You will need a ball of string, a metal or plastic ring $1\frac{1}{4}$ inches in diameter and a wooden toggle for fastening. Cut eight lengths of string each 8 yards long and knot these on to the ring. Using an extra length of string work over the uncovered part of the ring in blanket stitch. Loosen the knots and slip the ends of the extra piece through them, one in each direction. Tighten the knots and trim off the ends.

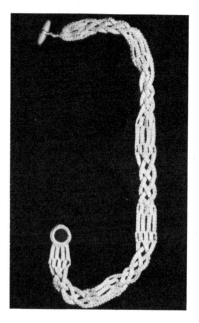

The belt is made throughout in flat knots, using a variation of the alternating knot pattern described in the next chapter. Start by making four braids of five flat knots each. ★ (Using the two cords on the right make a braid consisting of three double half hitches worked alternately, right on left, left on right, right on left. Repeat with the two left hand cords. Now make three braids of three flat knots each, thus joining the first four braids together.) Make a row of four braids of 20 knots each, using the same pairs as those used for the first row of braids. Plait these as shown in Figure 20A. Repeat the section in brackets, then make another row of four braids each with six flat knots. Repeat from ★ four times more, repeat the section in brackets once, then make four braids of six knots each.

Turn the ends under, glue down for about $\frac{1}{2}$ inch and cut off. Wind a piece of string round the center of the toggle leaving two ends long enough to make a twisted braid about $1\frac{1}{4}$ inches long. Thread the ends through the end of the belt in opposite directions, tie very tightly in a reef knot (Figure 20B) on the wrong side, glue down and cut off.

20A

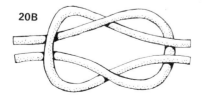

20B

Fancy belt with buckle

CROCHET ABBREVIATIONS:
ch. chain: dc. double crochet:
tr. treble: ss. slipstitch

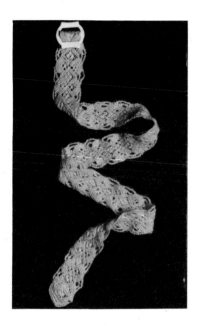

You will need a ball of crochet thread in your chosen colour, a small buckle with a center bar about $1\frac{1}{4}$ inches long and a crochet hook size 12. Start by making the crochet foundation as follows: make 13 ch., work 1 dc. into 3rd ch. from hook, 1 dc. into each ch. to end, 2 ch. turn. Row 2 Miss 1st dc. 1 dc. into each dc. to end. Repeat last row twice more, fasten off.

Cut 12 strings, each 8 yards long. Pin the piece of crochet to your pillow and knot one pair of cords to each dc. of last row. Work the macramé pattern as follows:

Step 1 Make a single chain of eight knots with first pair of cords on right and a single chain of four knots with second pair from right. Repeat with the two pairs of cords on the left.

Step 2 Make a flat knot using the four cords in the center.

Step 3 Using the sixth cord from right as holding cord make a slanting bar to the left using the next six cords. Using the fifth cord from the right make a slanting bar close to the previous one with the next seven cords. Repeat Step 3 in reverse with cords on left, so that the four holding cords meet in the center. Make a flat knot with these cords.

Step 4 Using first cord from bar on right (nearest top) make a double half hitch on it with each of the next four cords, thus making a bar slanting to the right. Repeat this using each of the next three cords coming from the long bar. You will now have four bars close together slanting to the right.

Step 5 Take the two remaining cords from the long bar and two from the last bar worked and make a double chain of two knots.

Step 6 Take holding cord of last bar worked and on it work a double half hitch with each of the next four cords on the left. Repeat with the third, second and first holding cords. You now have four bars curving round the double chain towards the center. Repeat Steps 4, 5 and 6 in reverse on the left.

Step 7 Make a single chain of 12 knots with first pair on right and a single chain of six knots with second pair. Repeat in reverse on left.

Step 8 Using right hand cord of flat knot in center make a bar slanting to the right with the next six cords. Using next cord of center knot make a bar close to the previous one, consisting of seven double half hitches. Repeat in reverse on the left.

Step 9 Make a flat knot with the two center pairs. Make a flat knot using right hand pair of previous knot and pair on right. Make a

flat knot using left hand pair of center knot and pair on left. Make a flat knot with two center pairs. This completes one pattern. Repeat Steps 3 to 9 27 times more. Work pointed end as follows: repeat Steps 3, 4 and 5, omit Steps 6 and 7, then work Steps 8 and 9. Using fourth cord from right make bar slanting to left with next eight cords. Repeat with fourth cord from left making bar slanting to right. Twist holding cords round each other once. Using third from right make bar close to previous one with next nine cords. Repeat on left, twist holding cords. Using second from right make bar with next 10 cords. Repeat on left, twist holding cords. Using first from right make bar with next 11 cords. Repeat on left, twist holding cords. Turn all ends to wrong side and sew down with matching thread, then trim ends neatly. As an added precaution, face the end with a strip of bias binding. Sew crochet foundation over bar of buckle.

These two belts are ideal for beginners. The fancy belt with a buckle fastening is made in macramé with a crochet foundation and the belt with a wooden toggle fastening is made entirely of flat knots

Alice band

The Alice band consists of a simple braid embellished with beads. Elasticated, it can be adjusted to any size

This is an attractive little accessory which consists of a simple braid embellished with beads. In the original these were about $\frac{7}{16}$ inch long but two or three round beads could be used instead. The braid is worked with cotton pearl thread number 5 and you will need 16 strings each 96 inches long. Pin a short piece of string to your pillow and knot the cords on to it.

Step 1 On eighth cord from right make a bar slanting to the right with the next seven cords.

Step 2 On ninth cord from right make bar slanting to the left with the next seven cords.

Step 3 Thread cords eight and nine through a bead.

Step 4 Using first cord on right make a bar slanting to the left with the next seven cords.

Step 5 Make a double chain of four knots with the two pairs on the right.

Step 6 On ninth cord from left make a bar slanting to the right with the next 23 cords.

Step 7 On eighth cord from left make a bar slanting to the left with the next seven cords.

Step 8 Thread eighth and ninth cord from the left through a bead.

Step 9 On 16th cord from left make a bar slanting to the left with the next seven cords.

Step 10 Thread 16th and 17th cord from the left through a bead.

Step 11 On ninth cord from right make a bar slanting to the left with the next seven cords.

Step 12 Thread eighth and ninth cord from the right through a bead.

Step 13 On first cord on the right make a bar slanting to the left with the next seven cords.

Step 14 Make a double chain of four knots with the first two pairs of cords on the right.

Step 15 On first cord on the left make a bar slanting to the right with the next 31 cords.

Step 16 Make a double chain of four knots with the two pairs on the left. Repeat Steps 7 to 16 18 times more, then work Steps 7 to 14. On the first cord on the left make a bar slanting to the right with the next 23 cords. Work Step 15. Work Steps 7, 8 and 9. On the first cord on the left make a bar slanting to the right with the next seven cords. Turn the band to the wrong side and pin a piece of tubular elastic across the cords level with the lower edge of the points. Tie the cords over the elastic in pairs using a reef knot. Trim off the ends and secure with a touch of glue. Remove cords from string and thread elastic through loops. Adjust size and sew ends of elastic together.

Making bags

five designs to choose from

Bags of all kinds can be made easily and quickly in macramé and are so hard-wearing that I am giving you instructions for making five different designs—two shopping bags, a handbag, an evening bag and a shoulder bag for a child. The shopping and shoulder bags are made from string in quite simple patterns. The other two are worked in finer threads and are more elaborate. Although they take longer to work they are, I think, worth the extra time and effort involved.

A useful everyday shopping bag

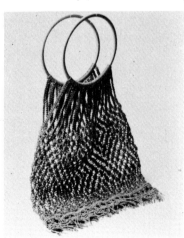

This was made from four balls of ordinary wrapping string bought in a stationery department and obtainable in pretty shades of red, blue, yellow and green. In addition to the string, you will need a pair of wooden or plastic handles 6 inches in diameter which you can buy in any good needlework shop.

Start by cutting 160 strings each 108 inches in length. Fix one of your handles to your pillow by knotting on two small loops of string and securing them with safety pins. Alternatively, you can fix them to the back of a chair or other suitable piece of furniture.

The bag is worked in two halves which are then joined. Knot on two pairs of cords to the handle and make a braid consisting of 20 flat knots. Knot on two more pairs close to this and repeat the braid. Continue in this way until you have worked 20 braids. The main part of the bag is worked in a very useful overall pattern of alternating knots. It is a pattern which has many variations and you will

A child's attractive shoulder bag that is fully lined and has a loop and button fastening. Instructions are on page 42

find more examples of it further on. It can be worked closely or loosely according to the type of fabric you wish to make. It can be worked from left to right or from right to left, whichever you find more convenient. Leave the outer pair of the first braid unused and make a flat knot with the second pair and the adjacent pair of the next braid. Make a second flat knot with the same cords (Figure 21A). Continue in this way right across the row. At the end you will have another pair of unused cords. There should be a space of about $\frac{1}{2}$ inch between the two rows and it is here that you can adjust the tightness or looseness of the fabric. Try to keep the double loops between the rows equal in size.

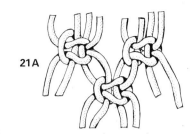

21A

Continue working rows of alternating knots in this way until you have worked 17 rows. Leave one pair of cords at each side unused each time, so that the number of braids decreases by one on every row. Make a second piece in exactly the same way for the other side of the bag. Pin the two sides to your support side by side. Using the pairs of cords left at each side complete the rows so that the sides are joined. This time the number of·braids in each row will increase. Fold the bag in half and join the other sides in the same way. This method enables you to work "in the flat" as long as possible and also obviates the need for constantly turning the bag as the work proceeds.

You will now have a tube hanging from your pair of handles and the bottom edge of this must be joined in some way. The simplest way is to work a decorative border. Pin a spare length of string across the base of the bag close to the last row of knots. Work a horizontal bar over this. If this seems to draw in the base work three half hitches instead of two occasionally to keep the bag the correct width. Join the ends of the holding cord as follows: when there are about eight or 10 cords left to be used, untwist the ends of the holding cord for about 2 inches, twist together half the strands from each and secure with a little fabric glue. Work the last few half hitches over the joined ends. Using the same pairs of cords as were used for the last row of braids make a row of braids all round, each consisting of four flat knots. Work two more horizontal bars close to the row of braids joining the holding cords as before. Be sure to make the join in a different place each time. To finish the bag sew the two sides together using a piece of string and a string needle. Work a row of running stitch between the last two bars,

Slightly more elaborate than the other bag designs, this handbag is made of both macramé and crochet, and has a bamboo handle. Instructions are on page 46

then come back and fill in the spaces left in the first row. Knot each pair of cords in an overhand knot and trim the ends of the fringe level.

If you would like your bag to have a base you can dispense with the fringe and insert a strip of crochet. Using the string and a fairly large crochet hook make a piece of double crochet 2 inches wide and long enough to fit the bag. Turn the ends of the cords to the inside, glue them down and trim them off. Slipstitch the crochet base to the last bar.

A third method of finishing the base is shown in Figure 21B. It is worked as follows: lay the bag flat on a table with the decorative edging towards you. Miss the first eight cords and make a braid of eight flat knots with the next two pairs. Miss the next four cords and make a braid of eight flat knots with the next two pairs. Continue in this way right across. There will be 12 unused pairs at the end of the row. Turn the bag over and work the second side in the same way making sure that the pairs used for the braid correspond with those left unused on the opposite side. Turn the bag inside out and tie corresponding used and unused cords together. In this way half the knots will be on each side. Turn the bag right side out and make a braid of flat knots using four cords next to one of the short braids. This braid must be long enough to reach the opposite side of the bag after it has been woven through the short braids. Make three more braids in the same way tying half of the ends at each side. Glue down the ends on the inside and trim off neatly.

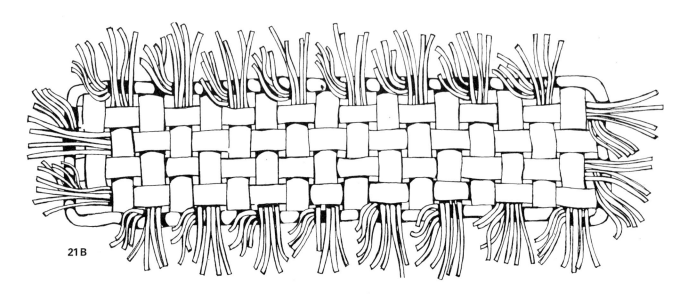

21 B

38

Shopping bag with leather base

This is a slightly more elaborate bag as it has a leather base and a more complicated pattern. It takes a ball of cord or twine, thicker than the string used for the previous bag, which comes in a variety of colours. In addition to the string you will need a piece of leather and another of skiver (leather lining). To make the base cut a piece of leather and one of skiver 12½ inches by 4 inches, as shown in Figure 22A. Glue them together and punch a series of holes all round, ⅜ inch apart and large enough to take the string easily. Cut a strip of leather and skiver 2 inches wide and long enough to go round base plus ½ inch and join the ends by sewing with strong thread. Punch an equal number of holes to those in the base along one edge. Take a 3-yard length of string and starting at one end thread it through corresponding holes in the base and side piece so that an equal length projects on each side. Using the left hand cord as a holding cord make a double half hitch with the right hand cord. Thread the holding cord through the next hole in the strip and out through the corresponding hole in the base (Figure 22B). Repeat all round, take the ends to the inside and glue down.

Punch 66 holes at equal intervals round the top edges of the strip. As they have to take a doubled piece of string they should be slightly larger than those punched in the base. Cut 66 lengths of string each 112 inches long and knot one string on to the strip through each of the holes so that you have 66 pairs of equal length. Work the macramé pattern as follows:

Step 1 Using each pair in turn work eight half hitches so that the braid twists to the left.

Step 2 Pin on an extra length of string and, using it as a holding cord, make a horizontal bar, working three half hitches with each cord instead of two. Splice the ends as described above.

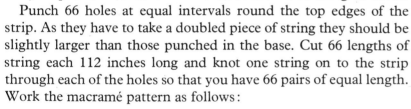

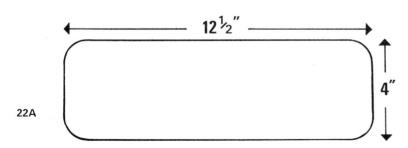

22A

12½″

4″

22B

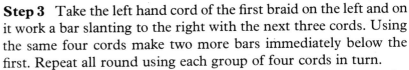

Step 3 Take the left hand cord of the first braid on the left and on it work a bar slanting to the right with the next three cords. Using the same four cords make two more bars immediately below the first. Repeat all round using each group of four cords in turn.

Step 4 Take the right hand cord of the first diamond (this was the holding cord of the third bar) and make a bar slanting to the right with the next three cords coming from the next diamond. Leave about ½ inch of cord between the bars. Make two more bars using the same four cords immediately below the previous bar. Repeat all round.

Step 5 and 6 As Step 4.

Step 7 As Step 2.

Step 8 As Step 1.

Step 9 As Step 2.

Steps 10 and 11 As Step 4.

Steps 12, 13 and 14 As Step 2.

Note that when working these steps the join in the bars should be in a different place each time.

Step 15 Make a single chain of four knots with each pair of cords. Take the ends over to the inside so that the chains form a knotted edge and glue down.

HANDLES Cut two lengths of string each 10 feet long and six lengths each 4 feet long for each handle. Lay the bag flat with the top edge facing you and measuring 4 inches from the right hand side of the bag, knot on two short lengths over the horizontal bar just below the second band of the diamond pattern. Knot on another two short pairs in the next space on the left. Work a twisted braid of 22 half knots with each set of four cords (Figure 5, page 16). Thread each cord in turn through to inside of bag between first and second bars at top of bag and back to the outside between second and third bars. Measure 4 inches from the left hand side and knot on the remaining four strings arranging them so that the long strings are on the outer side of each pair with the cord on the outside measuring 2 feet and the ones next to them measuring 8 feet. Work two twisted braids as before and thread all the cords through to the inside and back as for the first side. Now take all the cords on the right across to the left and the six short cords on the left across to the right. Tie cotton round them to make a smooth bundle. Using the two long cords on the left work over this group of cords as shown in Figure 22C, i.e., work a half hitch with each cord alternately. Draw the knots as tightly as possible until all the cords are closely covered. Take the ends through to the inside of the bag, spread them out fanwise and glue down. Work the other handle to match. Cut a strip of skiver ⅝ inch wide and glue over the ends.

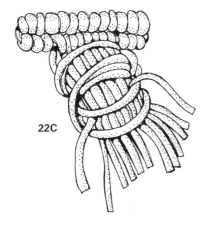

22C

Child's shoulder bag

Illustrated in colour on page 35

This was designed for a child and measures about $7\frac{1}{2}$ inches by $6\frac{1}{2}$ inches. It was made from the same sort of string as that used for the first shopping bag and requires three balls. In addition you will need a piece of matching material for lining and a button.

Cut 28 strings each 120 inches long. Pin a piece of the string to your support for a foundation cord and knot on the cords.

Step 1 Pin one end of another piece of string 27 inches long to the right of the cords and on it work a horizontal bar right across close to the knotting on. Make a single chain of two knots with each pair of cords. Bring the holding cord round and on it make a horizontal bar from left to right. Make a second row of single chains as before, then a third horizontal bar going from right to left.

Step 2 Using first cord on left as a holding cord make a bar slanting to the right with the next six cords, turn holding cord and on it make a bar slanting to the left with the same six cords. Repeat with each group of seven cords right across.

Step 3 Pin one end of a piece of string 18 inches long to left of work and make a horizontal bar to the right, make a row of single chains as in Step 1, then work another horizontal bar from right to left.

Step 4 Work as for Step 2 but start from the right hand side so that the "arrowheads" face in the opposite direction.

Step 5 As Step 3.

Step 6 As Step 2.

Step 7 Pin a piece of string 64 inches long to left of cords. This is used as a holding cord for the next seven bars worked from left to right and from right to left alternately, interspersed with rows of single chains of two knots arranged as follows: one bar, row of chains, two bars, row of chains, one bar, row of chains, two bars, row of chains, one bar.

Step 8 As Step 2.

Step 9 As Step 3.

Step 10 As Step 4.

Step 11 As Step 3.

Step 12 As Step 2.

Step 13 Pin a piece of string 80 inches long to left of cords. This is used as a holding cord for the next nine bars worked from left to right and from right to left alternately interspersed with rows of single chains of two knots each arranged as follows: (one bar, row of chains) twice, two bars, row of chains, one bar, row of chains, two bars, (row of chains, one bar) twice.

Step 14 Using eighth cord from left as a holding cord make a bar slanting to the right with the next six cords, turn the holding cord and make bar slanting to left with the same six cords. Make five more "arrowheads".

Step 15 Leave cord on extreme right to be cut off later. Using holding cord from last long bar (make three single chains of two knots each, make horizontal bar to left with these six cords, make three single chains of two knots each with same cords, make horizontal bar to right with these cords) twice, make row of three single chains of two knots. Using cord on extreme left as holding cord work left hand side to match, joining on a new piece of string if necessary.

Step 16 Using same holding cord make horizontal bar to right, row of chains, bar to left, row of chains, bar to right, bar to left.

LOOP FOR BUTTON Thread piece of string between last two bars just left of center, through from inside, over two cords and back to inside, make single chain about 2 inches long, thread one end through to outside, back to inside, tie ends and glue down.

GUSSET AND HANDLE (worked all in one) Cut eight strings each 8 yards long and a ninth 108 inches long. Knot on the eight strings to the base of the bag between the second and sixth bars and tie the ninth cord to the left of this to act as the holding cord. Make a bar to the right using the eight cords. Make a row of four single chains of two knots each. Pass the holding cord through a cord at the side of the bag, make a bar to the left, then another row of chains. Continue in this way, joining holding cord to sides of bag at end of each bar until knotted on edge is reached. Continue in pattern without joining, until strap measures 27 inches long. Continue in pattern joining gusset to sides of bag as before. Turn bag inside out, draw ends through, tie firmly and glue down. Turn ends of cords on flap to wrong side, glue down and trim off neatly. Line bag with matching material and sew on button to correspond with loop.

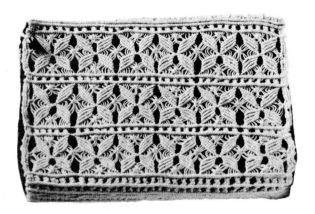

Evening bag

This was worked with a silky knitting thread. The pattern is quite a simple one which could be easily adapted for other purposes. In addition to the thread you will need a piece of buckram for stiffening, a piece of lining and a zipper.

Cut 60 cords each 84 inches long, two cords each 28 inches long and wind about 6 yards on to each of two cards. Using thin string cut eight pieces 11 inches long and two pieces 24 inches long.

Step 1 Place 64 pins in a straight line across your pillow about $\frac{1}{4}$ inch apart. When the cords are fixed the pins can be adjusted if necessary. Loop one of the long cords round the first pin on the left so that 14 inches hangs down on the inner side. Make a single chain of two knots round the pin. The rest of the cords are knotted on in the same way, using a short pair next to the first pair, then the 60 cords 84 inches in length doubled so that the cords are equal, then a second short pair and finally the second long pair knotted on so that the shorter end is inside. Using one long string as a foundation cord make a horizontal bar close to the knots, then turn the cord and make a second bar close to the first.

Step 2 Using the long cord on the left as a knotting cord work three vertical bars using the next three cords, turn and work back to the outside edge in the same way. Using each group of four cords in turn make a row of double chains of two knots each as far as last but one group. Using the long cord on the right work three vertical bars with the three short cords, turn and work three more. Using a short piece of string work a horizontal bar right across close to double chains.

Step 3 Leave first 10 cords, (make a flat knot with the next eight, using two cords on each side to make knot over center four cords, miss 12 cords) five times, make another flat knot, leave last 10 cords.

Step 4 ★ Using fifth cord from left as holding cord make a bar slanting to the right with the next nine cords. Make three more bars below this using the first cord on the left from the previous bar as the holding cord and using nine cords each time. Using 24th cord from the left make another diamond in exactly the same way, this time slanting to the left so that the holding cords meet in the center. Repeat from ★ five times more.

Step 5 Make a double chain of two knots with four cords on left coming from first diamond and with four cords on right coming from last diamond. Using four cords nearest top of second and third diamonds make a flat knot as in Step 2. Repeat right across. (There will be five flat knots in this row.)

Step 6 ★ Using holding bar of first diamond make a bar slanting to right with next 10 cords. Make three more bars close to this. In the same way make another diamond slanting to the left. Repeat from ★ five times more.

Step 7 As Step 3.

Step 8 Using first four cords on left work vertical bars backwards and forwards until band is level with double chain, with knotting cord on inside. With a crochet hook draw a loop of knotting cord through double chain, pass cord through loop and tighten. Continue vertical bars as far as lower point of nearest diamond. Work right hand side to match.

Step 9 Work a horizontal bar as before, a row of double chains and a second bar. Repeat Steps 3 to 9 twice more.

Step 10 Work a row of double chains as before, then work two horizontal bars close together using the second long piece of string. Turn the ends to the wrong side and sew down by working a row of double running stitches over the ends through the work between the last two bars. Make a second piece in exactly the same way and slipstitch the two halves together through the last bar on each side.

Making up Measure the piece of macramé (after pressing) and cut a piece of buckram $\frac{1}{8}$ inch smaller all round. Cut two pieces of lining $\frac{1}{2}$ inch larger all round than buckram. Lay buckram on wrong side of one piece, turn over surplus and tack. Turn in edges of second piece of lining to exactly the same size, tack over buckram and machine stitch all round, being careful to see that stitches go through buckram. Make two gussets from double material, each 2 inches wide and 1 inch shorter than folded up side of bag. Slipstitch a gusset to each side of bag, insert zipper and slipstitch macramé cover in place. Make a "puller" for the zipper either by knotting several strands of thread to form a tassel or by threading on several matching beads.

Handbag with bamboo handle

Illustrated in colour on page 36

This is a slightly more elaborate design than those already described but it should not prove too difficult if you follow the instructions carefully. To make it you will need a bag handle with a removable bar, five balls of fine yarn in your chosen colour, a spare piece of string of medium thickness, ½ yard buckram, ½ yard lining material, matching thread, a small piece of strong cardboard, a crochet hook, size 12, and a tapestry needle. The bag is worked on a crochet foundation and the sides and base are also in crochet.

3B

CROCHET HEADING Make 63 ch. 1st row 1 tr. into 4th ch. from hook, 1 tr. in each ch. to end. Fasten off. 2nd row Join thread to foundation ch. and work 1 tr. into opposite side of each ch. 3 ch. turn. 3rd row Working into both rows of tr. simultaneously make 60 tr. thus joining the two rows to form a tube. Fasten off. Pin crochet strip to pillow so that tube is at the top.

CROCHET ABBREVIATIONS:
ch. chain: dc. double crochet:
tr. treble: ss. slipstitch

MACRAME Cut 60 strings each 2 yards long. Knot on one pair of cords to each tr. of last row of crochet.

Step 1 * Using first cord on left make a horizontal bar to the right with next nine cords. Using 20th cord from left make horizontal bar to the left with next nine cords. Link holding cords as shown in Figure 23A. Repeat from * five times more using each group of 20 cords in turn. Link adjacent holding cords as before.

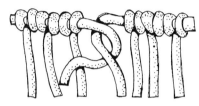

23A

Step 2 Work a braid of two flat knots with each group of four cords right across. Work four braids of two flat knots alternating with first five knots of previous row. Repeat with each group of five knots right across. Work three braids of two flat knots alternating with each group of four braids of previous row. Work two braids of two flat knots alternating with each group of three braids of previous row. Work one braid of two flat knots alternating with each group of two braids of previous row.

Step 3 Using first cord on left as holding cord make bar slanting to right with next nine cords. Make three more bars close to this using eight, seven and six cords respectively. * Link 20th and 21st cords and work bars with nine cords on each to left and right respectively. Work three more bars on each side alternately, linking holding cords in turn and working with eight, seven and six cords. Repeat from * four times more, then work four bars on right to correspond with those on left.

Step 4 Make a double chain of four knots with four cords on left. Repeat with four cords on right. * Using six knotting cords from last bar on each side of first pointed section make a flat knot, using two cords on each side over eight cords in the center. Repeat from * four times more.

From now on follow Figure 23B. Note that all flat knots are worked as in Step 4. Continue until there are seven rows of flat knots, and when this point is reached finish the pattern so that the bars form points as for the top of the bag. Note, however, that the number of cords used in each bar will increase instead of decrease.

Using the four center cords in each point make a braid of two flat knots. Work three rows of alternating braids as for the top having two, three and four braids in each group, then work a row of braids right across.

Using a piece of string as holding cord make two horizontal bars close together right across. Turn ends to wrong side, trim off neatly and sew in place with matching thread. Make second side of bag to match first.

SIDES AND BASE (all in one)   Make 20 ch. 1st row 1 dc. into 3rd from hook, 1 dc. in each ch. to end, 2 ch. turn. 2nd row Miss 1st dc. 1 dc. into each dc. of previous row, passing hook through both loops. Repeat last row until work measures 27½ inches. Fasten off. Slipstitch gusset and base between sides of bag so that top of gusset is level with lower edge of crochet border.

Work over seams as follows: cut two strings each 5 yards long. Knot to bag just below crochet top. Thread left hand cord into tapestry needle and, using it as a holding cord, make a horizontal bar with next three cords. Take holding cord through seam from right to left and repeat down the seam across the base and up seam on opposite side. Work second side to match.

Making up   Cut two pieces of buckram as shown in Figure 23C. Lay the smaller piece on top of the larger and machine stitch as shown by the broken line. The rows of stitching in the center form a pocket into which the piece of cardboard is slipped. Cut two pieces of lining ¾ inch larger all round than the buckram and cover the latter as described for the evening bag (see page 45). Oversew the two side seams and fold the gusset inwards. This will leave a small folded triangle at each side of the base which is folded under and caught down with a few stitches. Place lining in bag and slipstitch to lower edge of crochet heading and along top of each gusset. Make a braid of flat knots and slipstitch inside round top of lining.

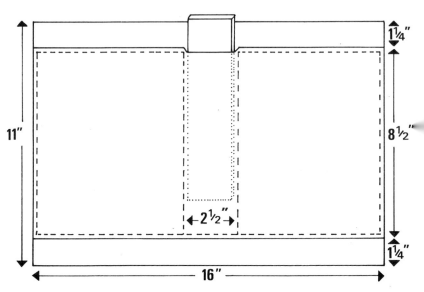

Decorative ideas for your home

Macramé has many uses in the home. Most of the designs in this chapter can be adapted for several purposes according to the type of thread you choose. The pattern for the brown and white cushion cover, for instance, could be used equally well for a stool top, chair back or chair seat. Both the designs used in alternate panels for the lampshade would adapt very happily for a cushion cover, lunch-mats or shopping bag. In most cases you will find that the repeat unit of a design needs only a few pairs of cords so that it is easy to make it smaller or larger as desired. You will notice that in this chapter I have introduced macramé worked in two colours and this obviously increases the number and type of patterns it is possible to make. Here again, the designs can be adapted quite easily. Some designs make use of three or even four colours but these need very careful planning to ensure that each colour occurs in the right place. You will find an example of three-colour work in the table lamp made from a bottle, while in the chapter on solid patterns there is a design for a table-mat worked in four colours.

Wall hanging

The original of this attractive wall hanging was worked in cream Novacord. This is a fairly thick cord with an attractive silky finish, although it comes in a rather restricted range of colours. It is usually sold for making knitted or crocheted handbags but it is just as good for macramé and is delightful to work with.

The original hanging measures 11 inches by 33 inches including the fringe but I have purposely designed it with a limited number of cords to a repeat. Thus, it can be made wider or narrower by adding or subtracting pairs in multiples of four, while the length

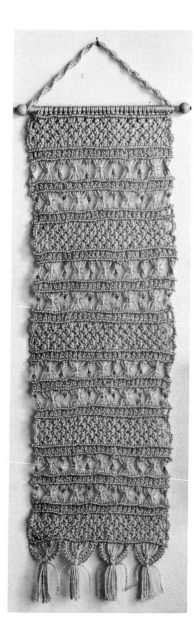

can be altered by varying the number of times the pattern is repeated.

You will need four skeins of cord, a wooden or metal rod 10 inches long and a pair of knobs in the appropriate material. Fix a knob to each end of the rod and tie on a piece of string so that you can hang it on a convenient support.

Cut 32 pieces of cord 6 yards long, two pieces 8 yards long and 26 pieces 12 inches long. The latter are used as holding cords for the horizontal bars. Knot on 30 6-yard lengths with an 8-yard length on each side next to the knob. The remaining two lengths are put aside to be used for the loop from which the work is hung. Note that each step is worked from left to right.

Step 1 Using one of the 12-inch lengths as a holding cord make a horizontal bar right across, leaving the ends to be fastened off later.
Step 2 Work five rows of alternating flat knots, one knot with each set of four cords. There will be a pair of unused cords at each end of the second and fourth rows and these are used to make four reversed double half hitches (Figure 13A, page 22) with the loops facing inwards.
Step 3 As Step 1.
Step 4 Make a single chain of four knots with each pair of cords.
Step 5 As Step 1.
Step 6 ★ With the first two pairs make a spiral bar of 10 knots, using the first half of a flat knot. Make two flat knots with the next eight cords, using the outer cord on each side over the six inner cords. Repeat from ★ four times more, then make a spiral bar with the last two pairs.
Step 7 As Step 1.
Step 8 As Step 4.
Step 9 As Step 1.
Step 10 As Step 6 but reverse the direction of the spiral by working the second half of a flat knot instead of the first.
Step 11 As Step 1.
Step 12 As Step 4.
Repeat Steps 1 to 12 three times more, then repeat Steps 1, 2 and 3 once.

FRINGE ★ Make seven flat knots with the first two pairs. Make two flat knots with the next four pairs, using the two outer cords over the six inner ones. Make a braid of seven flat knots with the next two pairs. With the left hand cord of the first braid and the right hand cord of the second make a very tight flat knot over all the cords between. Repeat from ★ three times more and trim the ends of the tassels level.

HANGING CORD Knot on the remaining two lengths of cord to one side of the rod next to the knob and work a spiral bar about 12 inches long. The center cords should be ½ yard long and the two outer ones 2½ yards long. Tie the ends to the opposite side of the rod. Turn all ends to the wrong side and sew down neatly with matching thread.

Patterned cushion cover

Illustrated in colour on page 54

This again is a very adaptable pattern in two colours. It is based on a design unit of seven pairs of cords. To make it you will need 2 ounces (50gm) heavy wool yarn in each colour, ½ yard burlap to match one of the colours and matching thread. The original was in tan and white with the burlap matching the darker colour.

Cut 28 lengths of tan and 21 of white each 4 yards long. Pin a spare piece of tan wool to your support and knot on lengths as follows: (one tan, two white, one tan, two white, one tan) seven times. Work from left to right throughout.

Step 1 Make a single chain of six knots with the first pair, * make a single chain of four knots with the second pair, a single chain of two knots with the third pair; miss the fourth pair, make a single chain of two knots with the fifth pair, make a single chain of four knots with the sixth pair. Make two flat knots using the seventh and eighth pairs. Repeat from * five times more, make single chain of four knots with next pair, single chain of two knots with next, miss next pair, make single chains of two, four and six knots respectively with next three pairs.

Step 2 * On seventh cord from left make bar slanting to left with next six cords. Make four more bars immediately below the first using the same seven cords. On eighth cord from left make bar slanting to right using the next six cords. Make four more bars immediately below this using the same seven cords. Repeat from * with each group of seven cords.

Step 3 Make three flat knots with each group of six tan cords, using the outer cords over the four center cords.

Step 4 Using second pair from left make a single chain of four knots. Repeat with second pair from right. Work remaining groups of eight white cords as follows: make a flat knot with the four center cords. Make a single chain of four knots with the pair on each side.

Step 5 On first cord on left each time as holding cord make four bars slanting to right using the same seven cords each time. * On left hand cord of center pair of white flat knot make bar slanting to left with next six cords. Make three more bars below this using the

Opposite:
A fringed table lampshade made up in panels of two alternating patterns. Instructions start on page 56

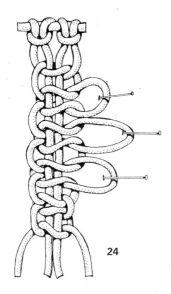

24

same seven cords. On the right hand cord of the center pair make bar slanting to right with next six cords. Make three more bars below this with the same seven cords. Repeat from * five times more. Using last seven cords on right make four bars slanting to left.

Step 6 Make single chain of eight knots with pair on outer edge on each side. Make braid of three flat knots with each group of tan cords as in Step 3.

Step 7 Work flat knots and chains with each group of white cords as in Step 4.

Step 8 As Step 2 but working four bars in each repeat.

Steps 9 to 14 As Steps 3 to 8.

Step 15 As Step 3.

Step 16 As Step 4.

Step 17 As Step 5 but work five bars in each direction.

Step 18 As Step 1.

Step 19 Work a horizontal bar right across on a spare length of tan wool.

BRAID EDGING Cut two lengths of wool each 24 yards long. Knot on to a spare piece of wool so that inner cords measure 2 yards and outer ones 10 yards. Work a braid of flat knots with picots down one side as shown in Figure 24. Make up cushion cover to same size as macramé panel and sew on braid all round.

Waste paper basket

Illustrated in colour on page 54

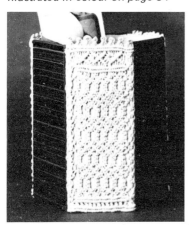

This is a simple design which consists of panels of macramé alternating with panels of plain fabric. To make it you will need a ball of thin string—yellow was used in the original—some kind of curtain or upholstery fabric, lining material for the macramé panels and ½ yard self-adhesive lining for inside the basket. For the foundation you will need six pieces of strong cardboard each 9 inches by 4 inches and a hexagonal piece for the base with each side measuring 4 inches.

MACRAME PANELS (make three) Cut 16 lengths of string, each 7 yards long for each panel. Pin 16 strings in pairs to your support and make a border of double chains as shown in Figure 17B, page 25.

Step 1 Using first cord on the left as a holding bar make a horizontal bar right across using all the cords. Leave the holding bar and use the next cord on the right to make a horizontal bar to the left just below the first one.

Step 2 Using the first cord on the left make a reversed double half hitch over the next two cords. Using the next cord on the left make a reversed double half hitch over the same two cords (Figure 13C, page 22).* On the fifth cord from the left make a bar slanting to the right with the next three cords. On the 12th cord from the left make a bar slanting to the left with the next seven cords. On the 13th cord from the left make a bar slanting to the right with the next three cords. Make a flat knot using a pair of cords from each of the last two bars. On the fourth cord from the top of the long bar make a bar slanting to the right using the next three cords. Using the next group of eight cords make a long bar to the left, then a short bar to the right with the next group. Join with a flat knot as before and complete the crosses. Using last four cords make four reversed double half hitches, facing alternately in each direction.

Step 3 Make two more reversed double half hitches on left hand side, then using fourth cord as a holding cord make a horizontal bar right across. Using fourth cord from right as holding cord make a bar right across to left. (Holding cord from first bar is used to make first double half hitch on second bar.)

Step 4 Make two reversed double half hitches on each side. Make a flat knot with each of next six groups of four cords each. Join fourth and fifth cords from each side as shown in Figure 25 and work four more alternating reversed double half hitches on each side.

Step 5 Work a row of alternating flat knots joining knots of previous row. Work a row of braids each of three flat knots joining knots of previous row. Join to border on each side as before. Work three more reversed double half hitches on each side. Work a row of single flat knots joining braids of previous row.

Repeat Steps 4 and 5 four times more, then work one more row of alternating flat knots. Work two more horizontal bars as in Step 3. Make two reversed double half hitches on each side and use each of the centre pairs to make a single chain of two knots. To complete, work two more horizontal bars to match those at the top of the panel.

Making up Cut three pieces of lining and three of upholstery fabric each measuring 11 inches by 6 inches. Cover each piece of cardboard with a piece of material glueing the surplus over on to the inside. Oversew the sections together along each long side, lining and fabric alternately. Bind the edge of the base with a strip of lining 2 inches wide and sew the base to the sides. Line with contact adhesive and stick a piece of the same over the outside of the base. Glue the macramé panels in place over the lining panels.

Opposite:
Braid edging completes this attractive, two-colour, patterned cushion cover. Instructions are on page 51

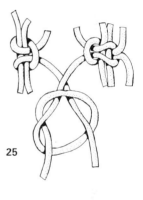

25

Opposite:
A multi-coloured table-mat design that can easily be adapted to make a stool top or chair seat. Instructions start on page 75

An hexagonal wastepaper basket with alternating panels of macramé and plain fabric. Instructions start on page 52

Two lampshades and a lamp base

These are articles which can be made very successfully in macramé and I am including one of each here. I feel, however, that as a general rule a patterned shade looks better with a plain lampstand while a patterned stand is shown to better advantage if the shade is plain. Thus the first lampshade for which instructions are given below was designed to complement a plain stand. The shade which accompanies the stand worked in Raffene (artificial raffia) over a glass bottle was bought in an electrical shop and is made in plain parchment. The original braid was removed and a simple braid and fringe in macramé added to bring the shade into harmony with the stand.

Smart table lampshade

Illustrated in colour on page 53

This was made from two hanks of rayon knitting cotton with a silky finish, on a six-sided wire frame 9 inches high and about 26 inches in diameter. It has two different patterns worked in alternate sections although you could, of course, use one or the other for all the panels. Again, the designs are adaptable ones, being based on units of eight and 10 cords respectively.

Start by binding over all the wires on the frame with narrow tape or bias binding. Cut 20 strings each 8 yards long for each section.

FIRST PANEL Knot on two strings close to first upright and on the right of it. Work a scallop as shown in Figure 18, page 25) with the first pair. Note that there is only one pair between the two sides of the scallop instead of three. Knot on more pairs two at a time until there are 10 scallops along the top edge and 40 cords hanging down, between the first and second struts.

Work a horizontal bar right across over the wire. Tie a piece of string right round the frame just below the bar so that it goes behind the struts of the panel being worked but in front of the remaining struts. (As each panel is worked untie the string, pass it

Made in a design that can be adapted to cover a bottle of almost any shape, this decorative table lamp base is worked with Raffene. Instructions are on page 60

A plain, parchment shade decorated with braid edgings and a fringe. Instructions are on page 59

behind the next strut and retie it. When the last panel is reached, join it by splicing and work the last bar over the join.)

Step 1 Make a horizontal bar over the string.

Step 2 On the fourth cord make a bar slanting to the left with the next three cords. Make a second bar below this using the fourth cord (formerly the third) with the next two cords. Again using the fourth cord, make a bar below the previous one using only one cord. Using the same holding cord as that used for the first bar, make a bar slanting to the right with the next three cords. Using the next group of four cords make a similar semi-circle in reverse so that the first three bars slant to the right and the fourth one slants to the left. Make a flat knot using the inner pair from each semi-circle. Repeat Step 2 with each group of eight cords right across.

Step 3 Work a double half hitch on the second cord with the first cord. Pass the holding cord round the strut from back to front and work another double half hitch on it with same cord as before. * On lower cord from second semi-circle make a double half hitch with upper cord. On lower cord from third semi-circle make a bar slanting to the left with next three cords. On lower of next two cords on right make a double half hitch with upper cord. Repeat from * three times more, then join to strut on right as for strut on left. This completes one pattern. Repeat Steps 2 and 3 11 times more. Tie a piece of string round frame as before and work a horizontal bar over it. Note that in this case the string remains outside the struts and is joined as before when the last section is reached.

BORDER * Using first cord on the right make a bar slanting to the left with the next seven cords. Repeat from * with each group of eight cords. On fourth from right make a bar slanting to the right with next three cords. * On fourth cord from top of next bar make a bar slanting to the right with next seven cords. Repeat from * with remaining groups of eight cords. Work a horizontal bar over the lower edge of the frame.

SECOND PANEL This is worked in the next section of the frame with the holding cords which attach it to the struts being passed round the struts between the cords joining the first section to the frame. Work scallop border and two horizontal bars as for first panel.

Step 1 (Miss three cords, make flat knot with next four, miss three cords) four times.

Step 2 On first cord make a bar slanting to the right with next four cords. On 10th cord make a bar slanting to the left with next four cords. Using last cord of first group of 10 and first cord of next make single chain of six knots. Repeat twice more with remaining groups.

Step 3 Using same holding cord, continue first bar of Step 2 with next four cords. On the fifth cord from the left make a bar slanting to the left with next four cords. Repeat with remaining groups of 10 cords. Repeat Step 1, take holding cord of bar on each side round nearest strut, then work Steps 2 and 3. Continue in pattern until there are $11\frac{1}{2}$ diamonds containing a flat knot down each side. Work horizontal bar over string, then work border as for first design.

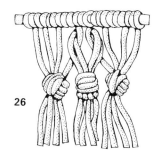

26

BRAID COVERING STRUTS Cut four strings each 8 yards long for each strut. Knot on four pairs to top of first strut. Use first pair to make a scallop. Make a braid of three flat knots with two centre pairs. Using the right hand cord as holding cord make a bar slanting to the left with next seven cords. Take holding cord round strut and back to right hand side. Work a second bar below first and take the cord round strut again. Make a single chain of two knots with each pair. Repeat from the beginning to the lower edge and take ends over wire.

FRINGE Tie cords together in groups of four with an overhand knot. Insert extra pieces as shown in Figure 26 and knot as before. Trim fringe to about 1 inch in depth and tease out ends. Line shade with thin material.

Small trimmed lampshade

Make or buy a plain parchment shade. If the shade already has braid edgings remove these and substitute a braid made from brown artificial raffia. Work a braid of flat knots long enough to go round top and glue in place. Make a similar braid for the lower edge but knot on short lengths of raffia along one side to form a fringe. Trim the ends and glue round lower edge.

Decorative table lamp base

This again is an adaptable design which can be used for covering a bottle of almost any shape. The original made use of a long-necked sherry bottle and took two skeins each of Raffene (artificial raffia) in brown, yellow and white. It has a plain parchment shade in yellow with a macramé braid worked in brown. In addition to the bottle and Raffene you will need one of the special adaptors obtainable at any electrical shop.

The pattern is a simple one of alternating flat knots with two knots in each braid. Cut the strings as follows: brown – 12 strings, each 9 yards long; yellow and white – six strings, each 9 yards long and six strings, each 2 yards long.

Take a small elastic band about $\frac{1}{8}$ inch wide and slip it over the neck of the bottle as near to the top as possible. Knot the strings on to this as follows: (9-yard lengths) (two brown, two yellow, two brown, two white) three times.

Work in the braid of alternating flat knots described above, pulling each knot so that the work lies tightly round the neck of the bottle and the knots are touching each other. As the bottle widens, work the knots a little farther apart. When the shoulder of the bottle is reached, knot on the six 2-yard lengths, as shown in Figure 27, yellow on yellow and white on white. Note that this must be done on a row in which all the flat knots are worked in one colour. On the next row make the flat knots using the new cords with the brown pairs next to them. Continue in pattern adjusting the distance between the braids as necessary until a point about 1 inch from the place where the undercurve begins is reached, again finishing with a row in which all the braids are worked in one colour.

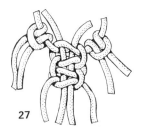

27

Tie a spare piece of soft string round the bottle and on it work a horizontal bar, splicing it to join. Using the right hand cord of one of the brown groups make a bar slanting to the left with the next three cords. Repeat with each group of four cords all round, then make a second horizontal bar as before. Work two rows of alternating flat knots with one knot in each braid then a third row with three flat knots in each. Cut the ends and secure to the underside of the base with self-adhesive tape. Cover with a circle of self-adhesive baize. Insert adaptor in mouth of bottle.

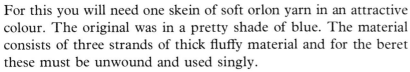

Attractive designs for you to wear

As you will, no doubt, have already realized, macramé can be used very successfully for making dress accessories. In this chapter I give you directions for making several garments using quite simple patterns. Again, the designs are very adaptable, since both the vest and bedjacket patterns could be used to make a stole or simple sweater. The beret, being circular, introduces something I have not mentioned before – the addition of extra cords to a design.

Town or country beret

Illustrated in colour on page 71

For this you will need one skein of soft orlon yarn in an attractive colour. The original was in a pretty shade of blue. The material consists of three strands of thick fluffy material and for the beret these must be unwound and used singly.

Cut eight strings, each 2 yards long and 16 strings, each 1½ yards long. Make a small ring by twisting up a few inches of wool and pin it to your support. Knot on eight pairs of cords in reverse using the 2-yard lengths and adjust the size of the ring by pulling the ends gently before cutting them off.

Step 1 Make four rows of alternating flat knots, making the loops between them a little longer each time to keep the work flat.

Step 2 Take a separate length of wool and pin down one end just below the last row of knots. Using it as a holding cord work a horizontal bar all round twisting the ends and working the last few double half hitches over them. The knots from the cords will not quite cover the holding cord and should be arranged so that there is a space between each two pairs.

Step 3 Using the 16 shorter lengths knot one pair on to each space. Work three rows of alternating flat knots as before, again adjusting the size of the loops to keep the work flat.

Step 4 Take a separate piece of wool and make another horizontal bar all round as follows: with outer cords from each flat knot make three double half hitches; with inner cords make two double half hitches.

Step 5 Using the inner pair of cords from one of the flat knots tie together in an overhand knot close to the horizontal bar. Repeat with each pair all round.

Step 6 Make another horizontal bar all round, this time working only two double half hitches with each cord, and drawing the work in slightly.

Step 7 Turn the work over and work three more rows of alternating flat knots as before, this time making the knots a little closer together on each row so that the work becomes smaller.

Step 8 Work two more horizontal bars close together each on a separate length of wool. Before cutting off the ends of the last foundation cord try on the beret and adjust the size by pulling the ends gently.

Step 9 Trim off the ends of the foundation cords. Turn in the ends of the cords to the wrong side and sew down with matching thread. Trim ends level and cover with a strip of bias binding.

Fringed vest

Illustrated in colour on page 17

This useful little garment is worked in strips which are afterwards joined together with crochet. It consists of a back panel, two shoulder panels, two side and two front panels. It takes three skeins of vest cotton which, although it is available in white only, can be dyed very successfully. The pattern is a very simple one consisting of only two rows repeated for the length required. It will fit a 34-inch bust, but can be made larger by adding one pattern (four pairs of cords) to the back panel. It measures 24 inches from the shoulder including fringe. To make a longer vest add 6 inches to every string for every extra pattern required. You will need four skeins for the larger size.

CENTER BACK PANEL Using a fairly thick crochet hook, make 52 ch. Cut 26 strings each $7\frac{1}{4}$ yards long (A) and 26 strings $4\frac{1}{4}$ yards long (B). Pin the crochet foundation to your support and knot on the strings in the following order: (ABBA) 13 times.

Step 1 Miss first four pairs on left, make second half of flat knot with next four pairs, using two outer pairs over two center pairs; (make flat knot in the same way with next four pairs) nine times, make half flat knot with next four pairs, miss last four pairs.

Step 2 Make a single chain of 10 knots with first pair on left, *
make a double chain of three knots with next two pairs, make a
single chain of five knots with each of next two pairs, join them with
half a flat knot, make a single chain of five knots with each pair;
repeat from * 11 times more, make double chain of three knots with
next two pairs, make single chain of 10 knots with last pair.

Step 3 Make a flat knot with each group of four pairs in turn.
Repeat Steps 2 and 3 26 times more.

FRONT SHOULDER PANELS Pin back panel to support
with foundation chain facing you.

RIGHT PANEL (This is worked on left side of back as it is facing
you.) Cut eight strings as (A) and eight as (B) as for back. Knot on
as for back, to first 16 sts. of foundation chain.

Step 1 As for first 16 pairs on back. Continue in pattern as for
back until there are 27 single chains on each side.

LEFT PANEL Cut strings as for right panel and knot on to last
16 sts. of foundation chain. Work as for right panel.

SIDE PANELS (work two) Make 16 ch. Pin to support.

Step 1 Make a flat knot with the first four pairs, make a single
chain of three knots with next pair, make a double chain of three
knots with next two pairs; make a single chain of three knots with
each of next two pairs, make a double chain of three knots with
next two pairs, make a single chain of three knots with next pair,
make a flat knot with next four pairs.

Step 2 Make a single chain of 10 knots with first pair, make a
double chain of three knots with next two pairs, make a single chain
of five knots with next pair, join with half a flat knot to chain of
three knots on previous row, make a single chain of five knots with
each of these pairs; miss double chain of previous row, join next
two chains of three knots with half a flat knot, make a single chain
of five knots with each pair; miss next double chain and single
chain of three knots, make single chain of five knots with next pair,
join to chain just missed with half a flat knot, make single chain of
five knots with each pair, make a double chain of three knots with
next two pairs, make single chain of 10 knots with last pair.
Continue in pattern as for back until there are 17 single chains of 10
knots down each side.

FRONT PANELS (make two) Make 12 ch. Pin to support. Cut
six strings each $5\frac{1}{4}$ yards long and six strings each $3\frac{1}{4}$ yards long.
Knot on to foundation chain as for back panel.

CROCHET ABBREVIATIONS:
ch. chain: dc. double crochet:
tr. treble: ss. slipstitch

Step 1 Make a flat knot with each group of four pairs. Continue in pattern as for back until there are 21 single chains of 10 knots down each side.

Making up Join thread to last single chain on right hand side of back. Work in crochet as follows: 2 ch. 1 dc. into corresponding chain on one side panel, 2 ch. 1 dc. into next chain on back. Continue in this way as far as top of side panel, fasten off. Join thread to last chain on opposite side of same side panel and join to front shoulder panel in the same way. Do not fasten off.

Continue round armhole as follows: (3 ch. 1 dc.) into each single chain round armhole. 3 ch. turn. Work (3 tr. into dc. 3 tr. into next space) all round, work 1 tr. into each stitch of foundation chain on side panel.

Join second side panel to back and front panels in the same way.

Still starting at the lower edge each time, join one front panel in the same way to each shoulder panel, continuing up side of shoulder panel as far as shoulder as directed for first row round armhole. Fasten off.

With wrong side facing join thread to last chain of left front. ★ 3 ch. 1 dc. into next single chain, repeat to top of panel, fasten off.

With wrong side facing join thread to foundation chain of right panel and work down to lower edge as for left panel. 3 ch. turn.

(3 tr. into each space, 1 tr. into each dc.) to top of panel, 3 tr. into end of foundation chain. 1 tr. into each ch. of foundation, (3 tr. into each space, 1 tr. into dc.) up side of shoulder panel, 1 tr. into each ch. of foundation chain across back, work down second side to match first, fasten off.

FRINGE Tie together two pairs of cords from each of two adjacent flat knots all round. Knot on two extra pairs at lower edge of each front to complete knots. Cut ends of fringe level.

Striped bed jacket

Illustrated in colour on page 72

This is an attractive little cape which can be made fairly quickly. It is worked in separate stripes, so there are not many cords to be coped with at a time. To make it you will need 3 ounces (75gm) double knitting wool in blue and 4 ounces (100gm) in cream, $1\frac{1}{2}$ yards ribbon, a pair of number nine knitting needles and a fairly thick crochet hook. The cape measures nearly 2 yards round the lower edge and has nine blue stripes and eight cream ones with the collar in cream. The blue stripes are worked first and the cream ones are then joined to them as the work proceeds.

FIRST BLUE STRIPE Cut six lengths of wool each $3\frac{1}{2}$ yards long (A). Cut six lengths of wool each $1\frac{1}{2}$ yards long (B). Pin a piece of string $2\frac{1}{2}$ yards long to your support. Knot on the cords to the string in the following order: A1 A2, B1 B2, A3 B3, B4 A4, B5 B6, A5 A6.

Step 1 Make flat knots using pairs A1 and A2, A3 and B3, B4 and A4, A5 and A6.

Step 2 Make flat knots with A2 and A3 as knotting cords over pairs B1 and B2 used together and A4 and A5 over B5 and B6 used together.

Step 3 Make flat knots with A1 and A2, with A3 and A4 over B3 and B4 used together and with A5 and A6. Repeat Steps 2 and 3 15 times more omitting the two outer flat knots on last repeat. Using overhand knots tie the cords together in groups of four. Work eight more stripes in the same way.

FIRST WHITE STRIPE Cut eight lengths of wool each $3\frac{1}{2}$ yards long and six lengths each $1\frac{1}{2}$ yards long. Knot on as follows between first two blue stripes: A1 A2, B1 B2, A3 A4, B3 B4, A5 A6, B5 B6, A7 A8.

Step 1 Make flat knots using pairs A1 and A2, A3 and A4, A5 and A6, A7 and A8. Take pair A1 through loop at side of blue stripe as shown in Figure 28A.

Step 2 Make flat knots with A2 and A3 as knotting cords over B1 and B2 used together, with A4 and A5 over B3 and B4, and with A6 and A7 over B5 and B6. Take pair A8 through loop on second blue stripe as shown in Figure 28B.

Step 3 Make flat knots with pairs A1 and A2, A3 and A4, A5 and A6 and A7 and A8. Take pair A1 through next loop on blue stripe. Repeat Steps 2 and 3 15 times more omitting outer flat knots on last repeat. Knot cords in groups of four as for blue stripe. Work seven more cream stripes.

Making up Slip loops off string on to knitting needle (220 stitches). With right side facing join cream wool to beginning of row and work as follows: (Knit 3 together) 72 times, (knit 2 tog.) twice. (74 sts.)

Knit 11 rows on these sts. Cast off.

Join blue wool to top of left hand stripe and work in crochet as follows: (2 dc. 2 tr. 2 dc.) into each loop to end. Fasten off.

Join wool to lower edge of right hand stripe and work to match opposite side. Sew center part of ribbon to wrong side of collar leaving an end at each side to form ties.

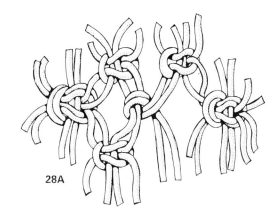

28A

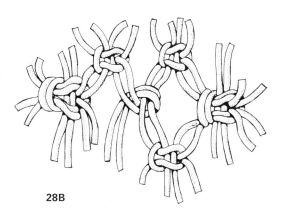

28B

CROCHET ABBREVIATIONS:
ch. chain: dc. double crochet:
tr. treble: ss. slipstitch

Little girl's poncho

Illustrated in colour on page 72

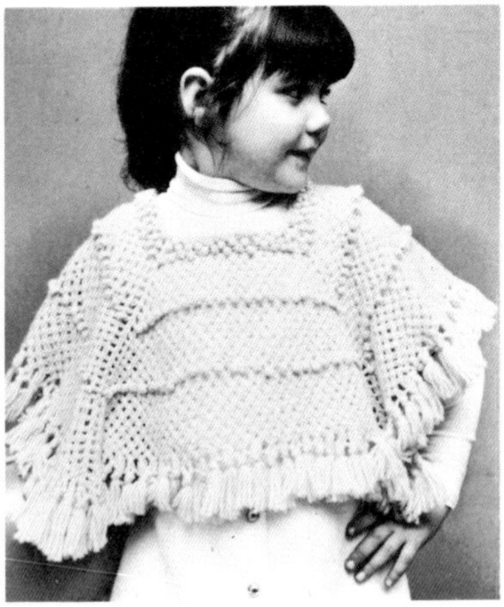

This is another very adaptable design which can be made larger as desired, either by using a thicker wool such as that used for the evening shawl described on page 68, or by working more rows of the pattern.

The original poncho was made from nylon quick knit but I find that usually this material is not so thick or bulky as similar yarn made from wool, so a garment made from the latter would automatically work out a little larger. The poncho is worked in four identical sections, the left hand cords for the second section being knotted on to the opposite side of the stitches in the foundation chain to which the right hand cords of the first section were attached. Section 3 is joined to Section 2 in the same way, while Section 4 is joined to both Section 3 and Section 1 to complete the circle.

To check the size of the child's poncho cut a paper pattern 23 inches square, then cut a 5-inch square in the center to allow for the neck opening.

To make up the child's poncho in a larger size, add 24 ch. to foundation of first section, 12 ch. to foundation of second and third sections, but note that fourth section remains the same at 24 ch. Cut six lengths of each of the following: 92 inches, 72 inches, 62 inches, 47 inches, 42 inches, 35 inches and 30 inches. Cut four lengths each of 25 inches and 20 inches in addition to 28 lengths of 96 inches.

Work sections as for small size but continue last band of alternating flat knots until all the cords have been used.

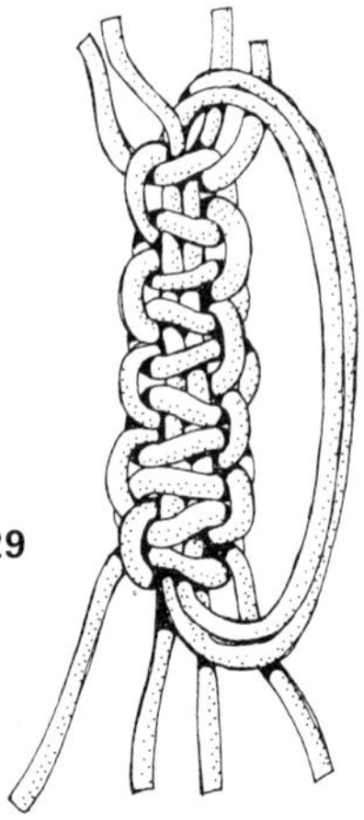

29

SECTION 1 Using wool double, make 136 ch. Pin center 24 ch. horizontally to your support with the remaining 56 ch. on each side sloping away at an angle. Note that cords are knotted on to each ch. of the center section and to the second and every alternate ch. down each side. As the cords diminish in length down each side it will be found easier to knot on each pair as you cut it.

Cut 28 lengths each 96 inches long. Knot on 24 pairs along center section and two pairs to each side. Cut 14 lengths each 90 inches long and knot on seven pairs to each side. Cut six lengths in each of the following sizes: 80 inches, 60 inches, 50 inches, 35 inches and 30 inches. Knot three pairs to each side from each group, starting with the longest and using each of the other sizes in turn. Cut four lengths 25 inches long and four lengths 20 inches long and knot two pairs to each side.

Step 1 Using 24 pairs in center make 12 large shell knots (Figure 29). Taking in one extra pair from each side, make 13 alternating large shell knots. Again taking in one extra pair on each side make 14 alternating large shell knots.

Step 2 Still taking in one extra pair on each side of every row work six rows alternating flat knots, followed by one row of large shell knots alternating with last row of single flat knots (21 shell knots).

Step 3 In the same way work eight rows of alternating flat knots followed by a row of large shell knots (30 shell knots).

Step 4 Work 10 rows alternating flat knots.

SECTIONS 2 AND 3 Join double wool to top right hand corner of previous section and make 80 ch. Pin first 24 ch. to support, knot on cords and work as for Section 1. Note that cords on left hand side are knotted on to opposite side of ch. on right of previous section.

SECTION 4 Join double wool to top right hand corner of Section 3, work 24 ch. join to top left hand corner of Section 1. Knot on cords to centre 24 ch. and to opposite sides of ch. on Sections 1 and 3. Work as for Section 1.

FRINGE Starting from one corner and working from right to left, take left hand pair from first knot, both pairs from next and right hand pair from next (four pairs in all) and tie together in an overhand knot. Repeat until there are 19 knots. There will be three pairs not used. Knot these with the double end from the foundation chain. Knot on a 10-inch length to end of foundation chain and use this as one pair to knot with next three pairs on second side (i.e., first knot and right hand pair of next). Continue knotting as before to end of side where there will be one unused pair. Knot on a 10-inch length to end of foundation chain and use this with end left on chain and one pair on right and left. Continue in same way along remaining two sides. Cut fringe so that each tassel measures about 2 inches.

An elegant evening shawl

This was worked in a simple all-over design based on a variation of the pattern of alternating flat knots. It took six 2-ounce (50gm) balls of thick wool yarn and the original was worked in white.

This can be made larger if required by increasing the number of cords knotted on to the foundation cord. Knot on the strings as directed until you have knotted on the 84 pairs for the first half. Still increasing as before knot on extra pairs in multiples of four—i.e., to increase by one pattern knot on 88 pairs before beginning to decrease the lengths; to increase by two patterns knot on 92 pairs, and so on.

As the pieces required vary considerably in length it will be found easier to knot on each length as it is cut rather than cut all the pieces first. Start by pinning a piece of wool 2 yards long to a convenient support. The cords are knotted on to this in a picot edging as shown in Figure 15A, page 25.

Cut the cords as follows: first length, 18 inches; second length, 15 inches; third length, 21 inches; fourth length, 16 inches. Continue in this way, knotting on as the cords are cut, making each odd numbered cord 3 inches longer than the previous odd number and each even numbered cord 1 inch longer than the previous even number, until you have knotted on 84 pairs. Note that the 84th pair marks the center of the shawl. Continue knotting on another 83 pairs, this time decreasing by 3 inches and 1 inch respectively.

Step 1 ★ Using left hand cord of first pair and right hand cord of third pair make a flat knot over the four cords between. Omit next pair. Repeat from ★ to end, ending with a flat knot (42 knots).

Step 2 Work a row of flat knots alternating with those of previous row using each set of four pairs in turn (41 knots). Note that the pairs in the center of the flat knots of the first row are not used in the second row. Continue working in this way with one flat knot less in each row until the row with only one flat knot is reached.

FRINGE Knot on a piece of wool 10 inches long to the lower thread only of each double loop along each side. Thread the end of the foundation cord through the nearest knot on each side and trim fringe level.

This elegant evening shawl is worked in a simple, all-over design based on a variation of the pattern of alternating flat knots

Making up a solid fabric

We come now to a slightly different type of macramé work in which the fabric is completely solid. Two methods may be used. The first consists entirely of slanting bars worked in alternate directions in a prearranged pattern. It may be worked in one, two, three or four colours and, although care is needed to see that the bars are worked evenly, it is no more difficult than any other type of macramé.

The second type of solid fabric is known as the Cavendoli technique and this is worked entirely in vertical and horizontal bars used alternatively. It is always worked in only two colours and the traditional way is to use horizontal bars for the background with vertical bars for the pattern. This is not, however, a hard and fast rule since I have seen patterns in which this order is reversed. The outside edge of a piece of work frequently has a picot border and to make this it is necessary to work at least one or two vertical bars down each side.

Patterns for this type of design should be worked out beforehand on squared paper but when doing this, one very important point must be borne in mind. If you draw a pattern measuring, say, 20 squares each way the macramé pattern worked from it will not be square but obling – i.e., longer than it is wide. It is difficult to give an exact ratio between the number of squares going in each direction, as this may vary according to the thickness of the thread used. As a general rule you will find that symmetrical designs work out well provided they are repeated in reverse only from side to side or up and down.

A comfortable and pretty beret made in a thick, fluffy material. Instructions are on page 61

70

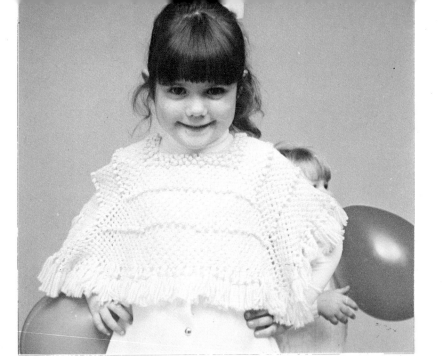

Curtain ties

These were worked in two kinds of thread, one with a silky finish and one with a matt finish, which provides a pleasant contrast. The original was worked in turquoise on a white background. In addition to the thread you will need two small white plastic rings for each tie.

Wind a long piece of turquoise thread on a bobbin. Cut 12 strings in white each 5 yards long. Pin a short piece of white thread to your pillow and knot on the white threads. Pin the end of the turquoise thread to the left of the first cord. Work two vertical bars over the first two cords, then work a horizontal bar using the next 19 cords, then make two more vertical bars on the next two cords, leaving the last cord to be fastened off later. Place a pin to the right of the last bar, take the cord from the bobbin round it to make a picot and repeat the row just worked in reverse. From now on follow the chart shown in Figure 30, keeping the two vertical bars all the way down each side and making a picot each time the end of a row is reached.

Continue in pattern until eleven "bows" have been worked. Work the last horizontal bar over a spare piece of thread. Turn the ends to the wrong side, stick down and trim off. Gather up each end of the tie with the spare pieces of thread and fasten these off. Sew a ring to each end.

30

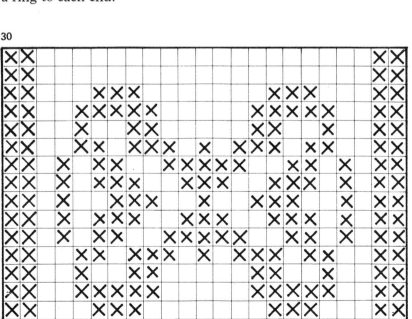

Opposite:
A little girl's poncho, completed with tassels around the edge. Instructions are on page 66

A striped bed-jacket finished with ribbon ties at the collar. Instructions are on page 64

A pretty compact case

This is worked in a soft thread with a matt finish, the original being in brown with the diamond pattern in white. As the two halves are sewn together there is no need for a picot edging except along the top edge.

Wind a long piece of white thread on a bobbin. Cut 20 lengths of brown thread each 30 inches long. Pin these to your pillow to make a picot edge as shown in Figure 15A, page 25. Pin the end of the white thread from the bobbin to the left of the brown cords and make a horizontal bar right across using 39 cords. Note that as the design requires an uneven number of cords the last one is left hanging to be used later for sewing up the sides. From now on follow the chart shown in Figure 31. Each square represents a double half hitch whether it is worked vertically or horizontally. The blank squares are all worked horizontally in brown while the crosses are worked vertically in white.

To finish the piece turn the ends to the wrong side, stick down with fabric glue and trim off neatly. Make a second piece in exactly the same way and oversew together down the sides and across the bottom.

31

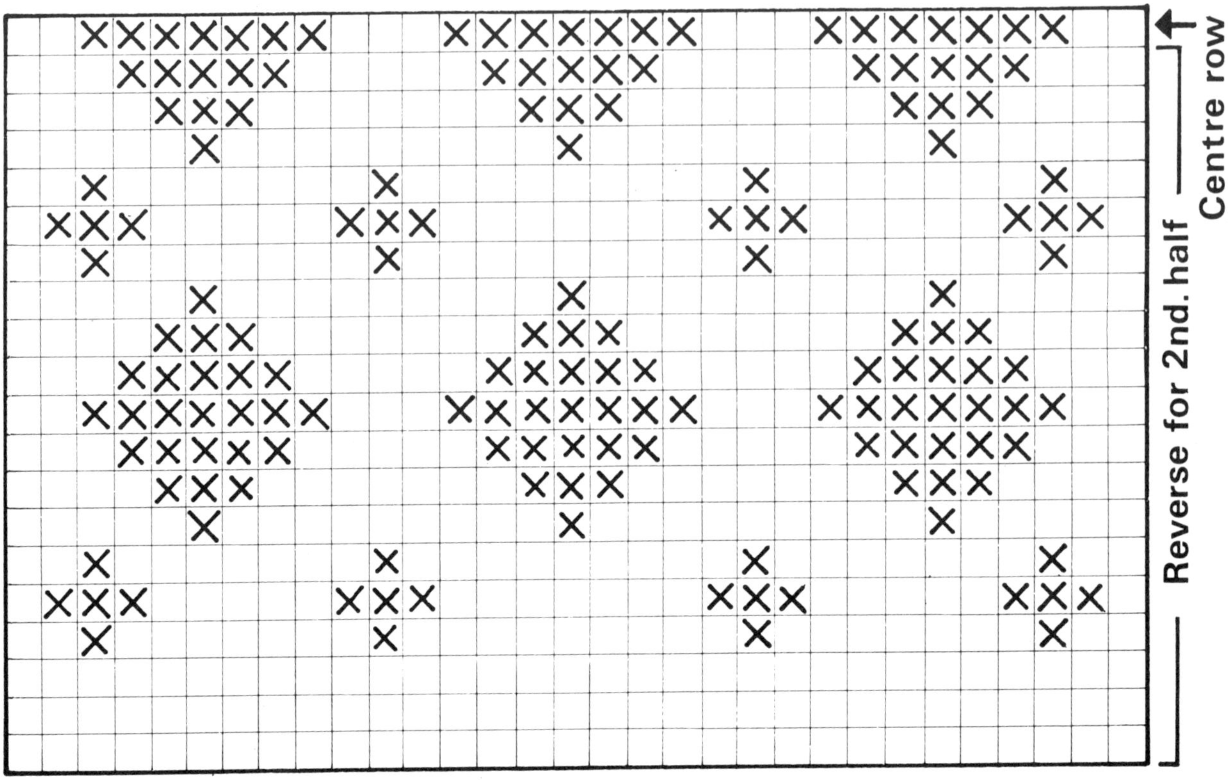

Multi-coloured table mat

Illustrated in colour on page 54

This attractive design is worked in four colours—red, green, orange and yellow were used in the original. It measures 9 inches by 15 inches including the fringe. Each mat takes 1 ounce (25gm) double knitting wool in each colour. The design is an adaptable one which could be used to make a very hard-wearing stool top or chair seat.

Cut the strings in 4-yard lengths as follows: 16 each, green and yellow and eight orange. Cut eight 5-yard lengths in red.

Fold each string in half and pin loops to pillow in the following order: (1 orange, 2 green, 2 yellow, 2 red, 2 yellow, 2 green, 1 orange) four times. Pin a spare piece of string right across cords about 3 inches from the pins.

Step 1 Work a horizontal bar over string right across.

Step 2 On second cord from left make double half hitch with first cord. On fourth cord from left make a bar slanting to the left with next three cords. On sixth from left make a bar slanting to the left with next five cords. On eighth from left make a bar slanting to the left with next seven cords. On 10th from left make a bar slanting to the left with next nine cords.

Step 3 ⋆ On 23rd bar from left make double half hitch with next cord. On 26th cord make a bar slanting to the left with next two cords. On 21st cord make a bar slanting to the right with next three cords. On 28th cord make a bar slanting to the left with next four cords. On 19th cord make a bar slanting to the right with next five cords. On 30th cord make a bar slanting to the left with next six cords. On 17th cord make a bar slanting to the right with next seven cords. On 32nd cord make a bar slanting to the left with next eight cords. On 15th cord make a bar slanting to the right with next nine cords. On 34th cord make a bar slanting to the left with next 10 cords.

Repeat from ⋆ twice more starting from 47th and 71st cords respectively, then repeat Step 2 in reverse on right hand side.

Step 4 (red stripes) ⋆ On 11th cord from left make a bar slanting to the right with 12th cord. Using the two red cords as knotting cords make a bar slanting to the right on each of next 10 cords (stripe will slope to left). On 14th cord make a bar slanting to the left with 13th cord. Using the two red cords as knotting cords make a bar slanting to the left on each of next 12 cords (stripe will slope to right).

Repeat from ⋆ with remaining groups of red cords. Note that on last stripe there will be only 10 bars. On second cord from left make double half hitch with first. Repeat with last two cords on right.

Step 5 (first row of four complete diamonds) On 12th cord from left (yellow) make a bar slanting to the right with the next 12 cords. On what is now the 12th from the left make a bar slanting to the left with the next 11 cords. On what is now the 12th cord, make a bar slanting to the right with the next 11 cords. Continue in this way working bars to left and right alternately and using one cord fewer on each side every time until there are 10 bars going in each direction, with four red cords meeting at the base. On two red cords on right make bars slanting to the left using two red cords from left. Work three more diamonds in the same way.

Step 6 (three complete diamonds with half diamond on each side).

FIRST HALF DIAMOND On second cord from left make double half hitch with first cord. On third cord make a bar slanting to the left with the next two cords. On fourth cord make a bar slanting to the left with three cords. Continue thus, increasing each bar by one cord until there are nine bars slanting to the left.

FIRST COMPLETE DIAMOND Start from four yellow cords at top. On top cord on right make a bar slanting to the left with top cord from left. On top cord on left make a bar slanting to the right with next cord from right. On top cord on right make a bar slanting to the left with next two cords from left. On top cord on left make a bar slanting to the right with next two cords from right. Continue in this way using cords from left and right alternately and increasing number of cords used on each side by one each time until there are 10 bars on the right and nine on the left.

Work two more complete diamonds, then work a half diamond on the right hand side reversing the directions given for the one on the left.

Step 7 Work red stripes right across as for Step 4. Work seven more rows of diamonds. Where red bars join on last repeat omit second double half hitch on second bar.

Step 8 (quarter diamond on left) On second cord make double half hitch with first. On third cord make a bar to the left with next two cords. On fourth cord make a bar to the left with next three cords. On fifth cord make a bar to the left with four cords. On sixth cord make a bar to the left with five cords. On seventh cord make a bar to the left with four cords. On eighth cord make a bar to the left with three cords. On ninth cord make a bar to the left with two cords. On 10th cord make a bar to the left with one cord.

Step 9 (half diamond) Work as for diamonds in second row until there are six bars slanting to the left and five bars slanting to the right. Finish right hand side as for quarter diamond and left hand side in the same way in reverse. Work two more half diamonds then work a quarter diamond on the right hand side. Pin a spare piece of string across work close to ends of bars and work a horizontal bar right across.

Knot the cords in pairs and trim to form fringe 2 inches deep. Press the mat with a fairly hot iron.

Macramé lace

working with fine thread

Macramé is not often considered to be particularly suitable for making lace but if it is worked with a fine thread it compares very favourably with knitting or crochet and with various types of needle-made lace. The illustrations for this chapter show designs for macramé lace used for a round doily, a Peter Pan collar and a square mat with a lace border. They are all adaptable patterns so that they can be used for a variety of purposes besides those mentioned. The doily, for instance, would make a delightful coffee table mat if it were worked in a thicker thread, while the mat edging could be used for other articles such as a chair back, tray cloth or linen blind. The collar pattern is based on a unit of only eight pairs of cords which makes it an easy one to adapt for a pair of matching cuffs.

Delicate doily

Illustrated in colour on page 18

As this is a circular design it must be worked on a pillow, preferably a circular one such as I described on page 10. In order to keep it a good shape it is essential to pin it down as the work proceeds and for this I find the pins with large coloured knobs very effective.

Make a paper pattern by drawing a circle 8 inches in diameter with several smaller circles inside it. (These are used as guides to help to keep the mat a good shape.) Divide the circle into 16 equal parts. The original design was worked in heavy stitching thread, but ordinary crochet cotton could be used, though in this case the size of the mat might vary a little.

Pin the pattern to your pillow then cut 16 strings each 1½ yards long. Wind a short piece of thread round your finger and pin it to the centre of your pattern as shown in Figure 32A. Knot the strings on to this ring and pull the ends gently so the 16 pairs are just touching.

Step 1 Work a double chain of four knots with two adjacent pairs. Repeat all round (eight chains).

Step 2 Work a braid of four flat knots with left hand pair from one chain and right hand pair from next, making the loops between the two rounds about ⅜ inch long. Repeat all round, placing a pin at the base of each chain, using the radii of the circle as guides. Cut 32 strings, each 1 yard long and knot on two pairs over loops of each space between the braids (Figure 32B). Make a braid of four flat knots with each of these two pairs, pinning down as before. There are now 24 braids.

Step 3 Leave a small loop on each side of each braid and work 24 braids of two flat knots each, alternating with braids of previous round. Pin down.

Step 4 Start with a braid in direct line with one of the double chains of Step 1. Use the left hand cord of the right hand pair as a holding cord and make a bar slanting to the right with the next three cords. Make two more bars close to the one just made using the same four cords. Using the right hand cord of the left hand pair make three bars slanting to the left in the same way. Repeat all round.

Step 5 Take the left hand pair of cords on one bar and right hand pair of cords on next and make a double chain of two knots, leaving a small loop on each side of each chain. Cut 48 strings, each ¾ yard long and knot on two pairs over each loop all round. Make a braid of four flat knots with each group of two pairs all round (48 braids).

Step 6 Work 48 braids of two flat knots each, alternating with braids of previous round. Adjust the size of the loops as you work so that lace is kept flat.

Step 7 Work 48 braids of four flat knots each, alternating with braids of previous step.

Step 8 As Step 6.

Step 9 As Step 7, still enlarging loops slightly to keep work flat. Cut 96 strings each ½ yard long and knot on to lower thread only of each loop (Figure 32C). Make a braid of four flat knots with each set of two pairs. Check pins to see that braids are spread quite evenly round mat.

SHELL BORDER Take the left hand cord of the right hand pair of one of the knotted braids of the previous round and using it as a holding cord make a bar slanting to the right with the next seven cords. Make a single chain of two knots with the last two knotting cords. Make a second bar under the first, curving slightly away

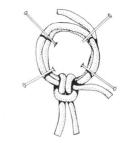

32A

32B

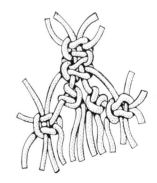

32C

79

from it and using the same eight cords. Make a single chain of three knots with last two knotting cords. Make a third bar under the second with the same cords. Make a fourth bar close to the third with the same cords. Using the right hand cord of the left hand pair of the same braid make four bars slanting to the left in the same way. Repeat all round (24 shells).

Fastening off Using reef knots tie the two cords at the top of the shell and the two at the bottom together letting the rest of the cords lie at the back of the shell. Using one strand matching stranded cotton sew down all the ends to back of the bars, being careful to take your stitches through each cord and not simply going over it. Trim off ends. Pin mat out to padded board, lay a cloth wrung out in cold water over it and leave until completely dry.

Lacy-edged mat

Illustrated in colour on page 18

CROCHET ABBREVIATIONS:
ch. chain: dc. double crochet:
tr. treble: ss. slipstitch

This consists of a square of linen with a macramé lace border about 2 inches wide. It takes a little over one ball of mercerized crochet thread number 30. Cut out a piece of linen 7 inches square. Turn in a single hem ¼ inch wide all round and machine stitch as close to the edge as possible. Trim off the surplus close to the stitching. Using a steel crochet hook work in double crochet all round over the stitching as follows: 83 dc. into first side, 3 dc. into corner, repeat all round, ss. to join.

Cut 89 strings, each 25 inches long for each side. In addition you will need 14 slightly shorter ones for the corners to be added during the working. Knot on one pair to each dc. along first side. Knot on three pairs to the center dc. of the 3 dc. worked into the corner. It will help if you knot the cords together loosely in groups of 15 pairs, ie 30 cords, as they are knotted on. Note that the corner groups have six pairs on each of two adjacent sides with the three on the corner itself to make up the 15.

Step 1 Work as follows with each group of thirty cords: on 11th cord make a bar to the right with next four cords. On sixth cord make a bar to the right with next eight cords. On first cord make a bar to the right with next 12 cords. On 20th cord make a bar to the left with next four cords. On 25th cord make a bar to the left with next eight cords. On 30th cord make a bar to the left with next 12 cords. Join four holding cords of top four bars with a shell knot worked as follows: make a braid of five flat knots. Take center pair through space between the pairs from front to back and work another flat knot to keep shell in place (Figure 29, page 66). Note that on corners half the bars will be on one side and half on the next.

Step 2 Make a diamond between each two adjacent long bars all round as follows: on fifth cord from top of bar on left make a bar to the right with next four cords. On fifth cord from top of bar on right make a bar to the left with next nine cords. On fifth cord from top of bar just worked make a bar to the right with next four cords. On fifth from top of remaining part of long bar on left make a bar to the right with next nine cords. On fifth from top of remaining part of long bar on right make a bar to the left with next 10 cords. * Using 10 cords from bar just worked make five single chains of two knots each. Using top cord of two remaining cords on long bar make a bar to the left with next 10 cords. Using last cord from same long bar make another bar with same 10 cords. Repeat from * in reverse on opposite side of diamond. Make shell knot with four holding cords.

Step 3 Work each corner as follows: knot on one extra pair to cord joining second and third bars of Step 1 (just above double bars at side of diamond). Make a shell knot on each side, using one pair from first shell knot with adjacent knotted on pair. Make three alternating shell knots using pair from bar on diamond for outer knots. Make two alternating shell knots joining those of previous row. Make one shell knot joining those of previous row.

Knot on one extra pair above each shell on outside of each of last three rows of shells (three pairs on each side).

* On top cord of bar of diamond on left make bar to right with next 12 cords. Make a second bar below first using next cord from diamond and same 12 cords. Repeat from * in reverse on right hand side. Join holding cords with flat knot.

Step 4 Work as follows between first and second diamond on first side: using left hand pair of cords from shell knot worked in Step 1 and next pair on left make a shell knot. Repeat with pairs on right. Using inner pairs from these knots make a shell knot. * On top cord from bar on left make a bar to the right with next four cords. On next cord from bar on left make bar below previous bar with next four cords. Repeat from * in reverse on right of shell knots. Join four holding cords with flat knot.

(Using four cords from last bar just worked on left and left hand pair from flat knot make three single chains of six knots each. Using next six cords from bar on left make three more chains of six knots each. Make flat knot over 10 cords with outer cords of outside chains. Make single chain of four knots with pair on right coming from flat knot. Make five single chains of six knots each with remaining pairs from knot.) Repeat section in brackets in reverse on right of right hand bar of Step 2.

Make half a flat knot to join single chains of four knots, then work

33

a chain of six knots with each pair. ★ Using last chain from diamond on left make bar slanting to right with 12 cords from six single chains. Using top knotting cord of previous bar as holding cord make bar below this with next 12 cords. On eighth cord from top of bar just worked make a bar to the right with next five cords. Repeat from ★ in reverse on right. Join center cords of last two bars on each side with flat knot.

Repeat Step 4 four times more then work corner as follows: work section in brackets to left of double bar on corner and repeat in reverse on right. ★ Using remaining cords coming from double bar on corner make single chain of six knots with pair on left, single chain of seven knots with next pair, single chain of eight knots with next and single chain of 10 knots with next. Using cord from single chain of four knots on left make a bar to the right with next eight cords. Knot on, in reverse, to holding cord of bar just made one extra cord between first and second chain, one between second and third and one between third and fourth. Using second cord of chain of four knots make bar to the right with next 15 cords. Make single chain of four knots with each of next eight pairs.

Using top cord on left (next to shell knot) make a bar to the right with next 26 cords. Using first knotting cord of bar just worked make a bar to the left with next 26 cords. Repeat from ★ on right. Join holding cords with flat knot.

Step 5 Make alternating shell knot on either side of shell knot at base of first diamond of Step 2. Make alternating shell knot between last two knots. Using top cord of bar on right make a bar to the left with next four cords. Using top cord of bar on left make a bar to the right with next five cords. Using next cord of bar on right make a bar to the left with next five cords. Using next cord from bar on the left make a bar to the right with next six cords. With next cord from bar on right make a bar to the left with next six cords. With next cord from bar on left make a bar to the right with next seven cords.

Using six cords on left and six on right make single chains of two knots each. (Two cords in centre are not used.) Using next cord from bar on left make a bar to the right with next seven cords. Using next cord from bar on right make a bar to the left with next eight cords. Using next cord from bar on left make a bar to the right with next eight cords. Using next cord from bar on right make a bar to the left with next nine cords. Repeat Step 5 all round.

KNOTTED EDGING Starting with right hand pair of flat knots at point of one corner make single chain of four knots. Take ends to back as shown in Figure 33. Repeat with each pair all round. Tie ends together on back of work using reef knots and taking one cord from each of two adjacent pairs. Cut off ends.

Dainty collar

This was worked with a white gimp thread but mercerized crochet cotton number 20 could also be used. Start by making a paper pattern, see Figure 34, page 86. Pin pattern to pillow or padded board.

Using a steel crochet hook, size 12, make 164 ch. Pin firmly along inner edge of paper pattern. Cut 164 strings each 15 inches long. These are knotted on in reverse to the crochet chain but there is no need to knot them all on at once.

CROCHET ABBREVIATIONS:
ch. chain: dc. double crochet: tr. treble: ss. slipstitch

Step 1 Start at the right hand side and knot on a pair to each of the first two chains. Make a half hitch with these two pairs. * Knot on eight more pairs. Using the first cord on the right make a bar slanting to the left with the next seven cords. Using the 16th cord make a bar to the right with the next seven cords. With the two holding cords make a single chain of seven knots. Make a single chain of six knots with the pair on each side. Repeat from * to the end of the crochet chain. Knot on a pair to each of the last two chains and make a half hitch with them.

Step 2 Make a flat knot between the second and third bars using eight cords, i.e., six cords in the center with the outer cords used for the knot. Repeat between each pair of bars to end.

Step 3 On sixth cord from right make a bar slanting to the right with next four cords. On first cord on right make a bar slanting to the left with next 11 cords. * Using cord on right of flat knot make a bar slanting to the left with next four cords. Using cord on left of flat knot make a bar slanting to the right using next 12 cords. On fifth cord from top of previous bar make a bar slanting to the left with next seven cords. Repeat from * to end working left hand side to match right.

Step 4 Make double chain of three knots with first and second pairs. Make flat knot with second and third pairs, make flat knot with third and fourth pairs, make double chain of three knots with first and second pairs. Make two flat knots alternating with knots of previous row, make double chain of three knots with first and second pairs, make flat knot joining knots of previous row, make flat knot with second and third pairs. * Using cords from second and third bars make a diamond of alternating flat knots in rows of one, two, three, two, one. Repeat from * to end, working left hand side in reverse to match right.

Step 5 Using holding cord from first bar on right make a bar slanting to the left with next eight cords. Using second cord from left of flat knots make a bar slanting to the right with next eight

Make this dainty macramé lace collar to attach to your favourite dress

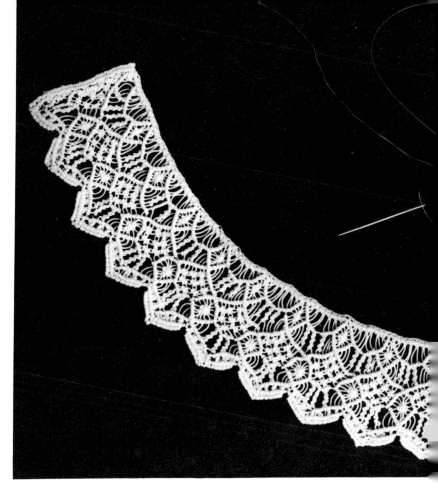

cords. Repeat from ★ to end. On right hand side make a bar slanting to the right with seven cords, then using first on right make a bar slanting to the left with three cords. Work left hand side to match.

Step 6 ★ Make a single chain of eight knots with holding cords on each side of diamond. Make single chain of six knots with pair on each side of this. Make flat knot with eight cords as for Step 2. Repeat from ★ to end.

Step 7 At right hand side make double chain of three knots using only three cords. Make single chain of six knots with next pair and single chain of eight knots with next. Using first cord on right make a bar slanting to the left with next three cords. Work rest of row as for Step 3 and work left hand side to match right.

Step 8 Make single chain of two knots with second and third pairs and with fourth and fifth pairs. ★ Make single chain of two knots with pair in center of angle between next two bars, make single chain of two knots with each of three pairs on left and right. Repeat from ★ to end and work left hand side to match right.

Step 9 Using first cord on right make a bar slanting to the left with

next four cords. Using right hand cord of chain in center of angle between bars make a bar to the right with next seven cords. Using first cord on right make a bar to the left with next four cords. Using first knotting cord of previous bar on left make a bar to the right with next seven cords. * Using left hand cord of chain in center of same angle make a bar to the left with next seven cords. Using right hand cord of chain in center of next angle make a bar to the right with next eight cords. Using first knotting cord of bar on right make a bar to the left with next seven cords, using first knotting cord of bar on left make a bar to the right with next eight cords. Repeat from * to end working left hand side to match right.

FRONT EDGINGS Knot on a string 9 inches long at right hand side between two short bars. Knot on a single thread $\frac{1}{2}$ yard long. Work two vertical bars over two short cords, taking knotting cord through inner edge of collar from front to back each time, as far as crochet chain. Work left hand side to match. Turn all ends to wrong side and sew down. Pin out on board as for doily.

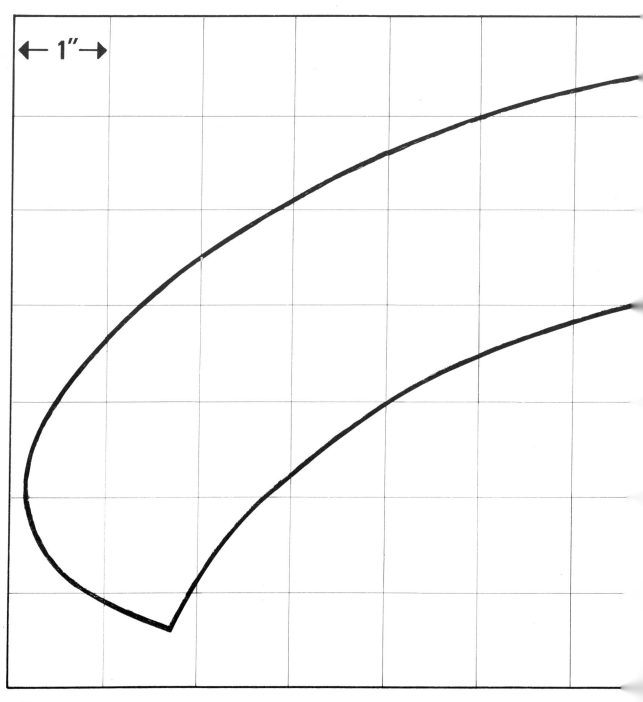

← 1" →

34

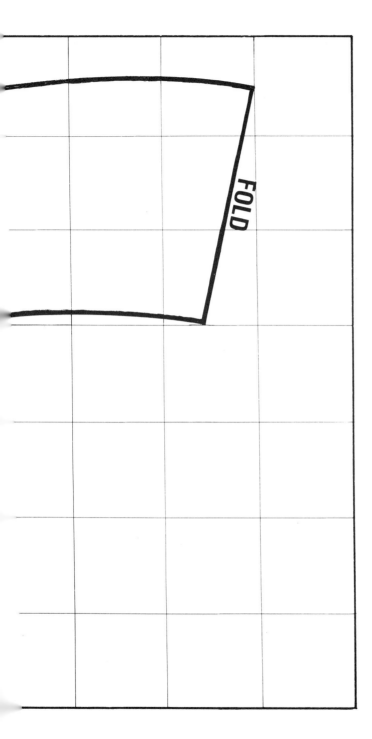

FOLD

Trace this diagram to make your pattern for the lace collar, instructions for which are on the previous pages

Index